CRUSADE & PILGRIMAGE

May birthday greetings
to
dear Marilyn
With love
From
Aunt Joey.

1987.

CRUSADE & PILGRIMAGE

A SOLDIER'S DEATH,
A MOTHER'S JOURNEY
& A GRANDSON'S QUEST

William Stevens Prince

Oregon Historical Society
PRESS

See pages — XIII, 38, 55, 109.

Library of Congress Cataloging-in-Publication Data

Prince, William Stevens.
   Crusade and pilgrimage.

Bibliography: p. 109
   1. Tuscania (Ship) 2. United States. Army—Transport
service. 3. Stevens, Percy A., 1899-1918. 4. Soldiers—United States—Biography. 5. United States. Army—Biography.
6. World War, 1914-1918—Casualties (Statistics, etc.) I.
Title.
D589.U7T877 1986   940.3'73'0922   86-5183
ISBN 0-87595-160-0

Cover: Illustrated are artifacts central to the *Crusade & Pil-grimage* story: High school graduation portrait of Percy A. Stevens; Laura Stevens's (Percy's mother) gold star (given to her by Bend's Shevlin-Hixon Company); her bronze medal issued by the U.S. government to each of the Gold Star Mothers during their later pilgrimages to Europe; a vintage American flag from the collections of the Oregon Historical Society. (Layout by Colleen Compton, photography by Alan Hicks)

Printed in the United States of America.

To all
the
Gold Star Mothers
of all our wars

CONTENTS

FOREWORD

A few years ago, I traveled to the lighthouse at the Butt of Lewis, the northernmost point of the Island of Lewis in the Outer Hebrides of Scotland. My wife and an enterprising companion had joined with me to view the equinoctial North Atlantic breakers rolling along the top of the world. Watching the waves crash in the autumn light, visions of ultima Thule, the ancient Greek conception of the northernmost part of the habitable world, came easily to mind.

We continued our travels down the coast. As we walked outside Stornaway, we crossed over a lonely point of land. There, in the mist, we saw a lone spar rising from the water. After some inquiry, we learned that the rusted steel mast marked the grave of a ship that had sunk with great loss of life on New Year's Eve 1918. Pressing through a raging storm, the British ship *Isolaire* was carrying a great crowd of eager soldiers home to Stornaway port. Most drowned within sight of their villages.

Later in the day we mused over the lonely, dramatic site called The Standing Stones of Callenish, one of the great megalithic sites of Europe, almost lost in but rising up out of the peat bogs that dot the western rim of the Outer Hebrides.

Although we were well past the season, we continued to tour the outer island. After leaving the country of Johnson, Boswell and Leverhulme behind we dropped down through the rain past North and South Uist.

Our random itinerary suggested that we were bound for Port Ellen on the island Islay, hoping to visit the lighthouse at the southern end of the Inner Hebrides, to match up lighthouses as the extreme ends of the Scottish island. Bad weather forced a change of plans and we were unable to extend our excursion. Yet, serendipitously, it was extended by other means.

A few weeks after returning to Portland, a manuscript came to the Historical Society that intensified my thoughts of the trip. I was not the only person pondering the secrets of the Mull of Oa and Kilnaughton Bay. On Oregon's coast, another's ponderings had become a completed story.

This manuscript revealed something far more dramatic, transcending my somewhat unfocused musings.

William Stevens Prince brought a dreadful reality back from the fogs that ever seem to temporarily screen events of a preceding generation. Because of his poignant account, the Mull of Oa and its towering, bleak relationship to the steamers *Tuscania* and *Otranto* will live in my memory. The story is heightened by its curious association with the American West, (colorful and crusty Harry Truman of Mount St. Helens fame was a *Tuscania* survivor) and with what was then the village of Bend, Oregon, such a very long distance from the deadly waters of the North Channel and the U-boat captains of World War I who fattened their reputations there.

The Society is proud indeed to publish this very unusual and well-told story of the short but meaningful life of Private Percy A. Stevens and the ramifications of the events in Stevens's life on those around him.

Thomas Vaughan
Executive Director
Oregon Historical Society

PREFACE

This book began as a sort of minor *Roots*, a search into the past of two relatives, my uncle Percy Stevens who died at eighteen in the torpedoing of the *Tuscania*, the first American troopship to be sunk by a German U-boat in World War I, and his mother, my grandmother, Mrs. Laura Stevens of Bend, Oregon, who was one of the more than six thousand Gold Star Mothers who made pilgrimages to their sons' graves in Europe in the nineteen thirties. But as my quest broadened and my research deepened, I began to see that their stories were not mine alone; they were the stories of many American families whose uncles and grandmothers (great-uncles and great-grandmothers) had also participated in the major drama of the first quarter of this century, the First World War, the "Great War."

So I have tried to tell not just my uncle's and grandmother's stories, and my quest too, but the larger stories as well, to show how another generation of Americans felt about the 1914-18 War, how they reacted to the sinking of the *Tuscania*, and how public attitudes following the War resulted in and brought about the Gold Star Mothers pilgrimages.

To some of us, living as we do today in a less idealistic age, our grandparents' attitudes toward war in 1918 and our mothers' in 1930 might seem like naive jingoism on the one hand and childish sentimentality on the other: as the author, I have tried not to judge them but to present them as I found them; objectively, I hope, but not without sympathy.

If any Gold Star Mothers are still living they will be approaching their centenary. The youngest *Tuscania* survivors will be in their eighties. The one *Tuscania* veteran I knew, and he only through correspondence, died in 1982, aged eighty-seven. If any of his shipmates happen upon this narrative they will be interested to learn that Captain Wilhelm Meyer, the commander of the U-boat that sank their ship, lived through the War, afterwards becoming a reserve officer in the German Navy. He served in an administrative position in World War II and married in 1942. He died in 1952 at the age of sixty-three. His widow lives in Bad-Neuenahr-Ahrweiler, West Germany. They had no children.

ACKNOWLEDGEMENTS

Like all histories, this one leans on the shoulders of a great many people. I want to thank especially the following persons for the generous help they gave me: Mrs. Josephine Evans Harpham, Santa Barbara, California; the late Mr. Islay Shanks, Port Ellen, Isle of Islay, Scotland; his wife Nett, his brother Alastair, his sister-in-law Flora; the late Mr. Edward T. Lauer, Secretary Treasurer of the National *Tuscania* Survivors Association, Wauwatosa, Wisconsin; Mr. Tim Epps, Port Charlotte, Isle of Islay; Mr. Hew McCallum, Girvan, Ayrshire, Scotland; Mrs. Catherine Pratt, Assistant Librarian, Department of Social Sciences, The Mitchell Library, Glasgow; Herr Christoph Terweil, Rhede, West Germany; Mr. Thomas V. Hull, director, the American Legion National Headquarters Library, Indianapolis, Indiana; Dr. Harold Langley, curator and supervisor, Division of Naval History, the Smithsonian Institution; Dr. and Mrs. Charles Hallett, New York City; Mrs. Louise Hamby, Bend, Oregon; Mrs. Ruth Lang, Mrs. Carol Boyd, Mrs. Dorothy Miller McCauley, Mrs. Frances Thompson, and Mr. Pat Cashman, also of Bend; Dr. Lawrence Willson, professor emeritus of English, University of California at Santa Barbara; Alan Hicks for his cover photography and John Tomlinson for his maps; Mr. Bruce Taylor Hamilton, who heads the Oregon Historical Society Press, and the staff: Denise Bekkedahl, Adair Law, Colleen Compton, Krisell Buxton, and Thomas Booth. Finally, I want to thank my wife Joan for typing the manuscript several times, for diplomatically calling my attention to misspellings and solecisms, and for being my ever cheerful traveling companion.

It goes without saying that I alone am responsible for any flaws in content or style the reader might find in this book.

Painting of Kilnaughton Bay by A. Shanks. (Author's collection.)

PROLOGUE

A Scottish friend sent me a clipping from the *Glasgow Herald*. It describes the plans of a British diver to carry out salvage operations on the *Tuscania*, the first American troopship to be sunk by a German U-boat in World War I, the "Great War," as my grandmother used to call it. This bit of paper, like the focusing knob on a telescope, sharpens three blurred landmarks in the distant landscape of my childhood: a colored print, a photograph, and a gold star.

The print once hung in my tiny bedroom on the second floor of the solid brick house I called home in the small central Oregon town of Bend. There is a blue bay and a beach, a graveyard on a green meadow and a white tower on a rocky point. "Kilnaughton Bay and Churchyard, Isle of Islay, Scotland," read the label at the top; and below:

Scene Near Where the S.S. Tuscania Was Torpedoed, February 5, 1918, by a German U-boat. This picture is a reproduction of a painting by A. Shanks, British Army officer, who was on the scene at the time of the disaster, and who has since given his life for the cause of Democracy on the Western Front. Some of the survivors were landed at the point indicated by the circle (near Port Ellen) and provided with shelter there, and many [casualties] were buried in the spot indicated by the **x** on the lower right side of the picture. Just to the left of the tower, and eighteen miles beyond, lies the *Tuscania*.

Down the hall from my room was my grandmother's. Here hung the photograph and the star. Whenever I crept into Grannie's hushed, lavender-scented bedroom, furnished with the bird's-eye maple bed, the oriental rug, the creaky rocking chair (her crocheted shawl thrown over it), I would stand and stare up at these two icons. The photograph now hangs here in my study. It is a fresh, handsome face—like Shakespeare's Viola/Cesario—"Not yet old enough for a man nor young enough for a boy." The photographer has not quite succeeded in air-brushing out the cow-

Percy's graduation portrait.
(Author's collection.)

lick behind the right ear. Did Grannie, I wonder, lick two fingers and try to plaster down those unruly hairs as my mother did mine? The boy wears a dark suit and a tie; this is his high school graduation portrait taken in 1917, three months before his eighteenth birthday. There was another, smaller copy of it on my mother's dressing table next to her silver hairbrush and hand mirror. Sometimes as I stood watching her comb out her waist-length auburn hair, she would pick it up and hold it in front of me saying, "This is your Uncle Percy. He was my youngest brother. He died in the war."

Next to Percy's photograph in Grannie's room was the gold star, two inches wide from point to point, framed and mounted on a background of red and white silk. Standing close I could read the engraving on it:

In Memoriam
Percy A. Stevens
Co. D. 6th Batl.
20th Engineers
He Answered
Humanity's Call
Feb. 5th, 1918

Gazing first at the star then at the photo I would wonder about this "uncle" who had "died in the war." Men, I knew, fought in wars. My father, Frank Prince, had done so. I also knew some men had died; but surely not boys the same age as my eldest brother.

If I had to pick a date when I began to realize that the print, photo, and star were all somehow

Gold Star. The gold star that was presented to my grandmother, Mrs. Laura Stevens, by the employees of the Shevlin-Hixon Lumber Company in Bend. This was their tribute to her upon the loss of her son Percy when the troopship *Tuscania* was torpedoed by a German U-boat in 1918. She sewed it by its points over the blue star that she had placed in the window of her home when Percy enlisted in the army. After the War she hung it on her bedroom wall beside Percy's portrait. Stars like these gave the name to Gold Star Mothers. (Reproduced actual size.)

connected it would be June 1930, just before I was eight. It was then that I knew the star was the reason why Grannie, who was seventy, was going on a long trip. For when I asked my mother why my grandmother was going (I did not want her to) I was told that she was a Gold Star Mother and that she would be going on a Gold Star Mothers Pilgrimage.

Now, fifty years later, the Scottish newspaper clipping has nudged me into making my own pilgrimage to discover how Uncle Percy came to be buried at the place marked **x** on a Hebridean island, and how that gold star sent Grannie on her six thousand mile journey to his grave. As with hers, my pilgrimage begins in the central Oregon town of Bend, my birthplace.

CRUSADE

Wall Street in Bend around 1918, much as Percy left it when he went off to war.
(Author's collection.)

SCHOOL DAYS

Today Bend is an overcrowded, restless city of over 18,000 inhabitants. When Grannie began her pilgrimage in 1930 it was a relaxed little town of 8,848. In 1917, when Percy graduated from high school, only 1,105 people lived in the frontier settlement that had been established less than twenty years before near the eastern slopes of the Cascade Mountains. Downtown, a couple of dozen merchants served the mill workers, loggers, and ranchers from wood-framed stores facing each other across Wall Street. Boardwalks kept shoppers out of summer's lava dust and winter's sticky mud. In the park-like woods near the river, most of the homes were built of native pine; a few were solidly constructed of the black lava tufa that long ago had poured out of the seven mountains lining the western horizon. One resident who had built up against a lava plain boasted that the back wall of his fireplace was thirty-five miles thick. Flowing out of the mountains, sometimes cutting deep canyons through the lava, was the Deschutes River, *Rivière des Chutes*, so named by French-speaking explorers for its numerous cataracts. Its cold, pure stream gave the residents their drinking water, irrigated their pastures, and generated their electricity. In 1914 it was filling the log ponds for the two saw mills then being built. By 1916 these mills, Shevlin-Hixon and Brooks-Scanlon, were converting the surrounding forests of ponderosa pine into millions of board feet of lumber.

It was the lumber boom that brought Percy's family west. In 1906, when he was six years old his mother took him and his two brothers and three sisters from their home in Minneapolis to Enderby, British Columbia. There they joined his father, Fred Stevens, who was a manager of one of the many lumber mills feeding off the vast forests of western Canada. The large family lived in a three-story, white clapboard house on a big lot surrounded by a picket fence. A snapshot of Percy, taken when he was twelve, is an ironic augury of things to come. Dressed in a sort of "Rough Riders" uniform—campaign hat, neckerchief, khaki shirt, breeches, and puttees—he stands at attention, grasping the muzzle of the rifle beside him. The Soldier Boy. That same year his older sister Mabel married my father, Frank Prince, who, in 1916, also following the lumber boom,

Percy's home in Enderby, British Columbia is in right foreground. The smoke is from the Rogers Lumber Co. Mill, managed by Percy's father, Fred Stevens. (Author's collection.)

Percy Stevens, age 12, as a soldier boy.
(Author's collection.)

Percy with his mother (Grannie), father, and two sisters Hazel and Mabel (kneeling), in Enderby, B.C. 1912. (Author's collection.)

took his wife and their infant son to Bend. By then Percy's middle sister and older brothers had either married or gone their own ways, so Percy, fifteen, went with his sister Mabel to Oregon. Either that year or the next, Grandmother Stevens followed with her youngest daughter, Hazel ("Nan"), leaving Grandfather alone in Enderby. Whatever caused this separation was hidden from me by my mother, who, ever conscious of reputation, always double-locked and threw away the key to any cupboard that could possibly harbor a family skeleton.

In 1917, Percy's senior year at Bend High School, he was manager of the track team, secretary of the Emersonian Society, class treasurer, on the student music committee, and cartoonist for the yearbook, the *Pilot* (named for Pilot Butte, a three hundred foot cinder cone on the eastern edge of town, used by pioneer wagon trains coming across the desert as a guide to the ford across the Deschutes River). A section headed "Athletics" features one of his drawings, a caricature of a football player. It is signed "Pike," his nom-de-plume and nickname. I asked Dorothy Miller McCauley, one of Percy's classmates still living in Bend, how he got the name, suggesting (from my own experience in growing up there) that in a small lumber town like Bend a boy with a name like Percy might have been labeled a "sissy." She smiled. "I don't know how he got the name 'Pike.' It does sound kind of tough, doesn't it? But he was no sissy. He *was* fine featured, almost like a girl. But the boys liked him as much as the girls did."

Sprinkled through the yearbook are tiny snapshots of the seniors at play: dancing, picnicking in

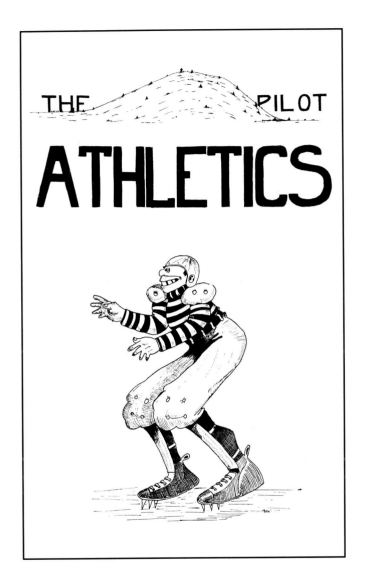

"Pike" Stevens' cartoon in *The Pilot*, 1917, volume one. "Published by the Junior and Senior classes in the interest of Bend High School." (Author's collection.)

HIGH SCHOOL
COMMENCEMENT
BEND, OREGON

Song, "Our Hearts Are Happy and Light" .... Adams

Girls' Glee Club.

Address, Rev. George B. Van Waters.

Piano solo, "Im Wundershonen Monat Mai" _____

F. S. Francis.

Awarding of medals and honors, E. P. Bolt.

Duet, "See the Pale Moon" .... Campana

Marie Brosterhous and Mary Linster.

Superintendent's report, F. Thordarson.

Conferring of Diplomas.

CLASS OF 1917.

Marie Brosterhous, Valedictorian

Ruth Vandevert, Salutatorian

Aleck Mersdorf	Dorothy Miller
Margaret Thompson	Mary Linster
Gertrude Reynolds	Rose Hunnell
Lowell Henderson	Robert Fulton
Evelyn Bedient	Mae Green
Florence Gilson	Percy Stevens
Frances Thompson	Hattie Dick

Ralph Curtis.

Bend High School Commencement announcement, class of 1917. (Author's collection.)

the mountains, hiking over the lava beds, hamming it up for the photographer. There are the "Class Prophecies" and the "Class Wills," the stuff of high school yearbooks then, now, and always. Corny and trite but not without truth, they are mini-parodies of personal idiosyncrasies. Did Percy's prophecy hint at some sympathy he had expressed for the Mexican guerrilla, Pancho Villa, who was then harassing Brigadier General John J. Pershing along the Texas border?—"Pike Stevens is Commander-in-Chief of the Mexican army, and you can well believe that it keeps him moving to hold down that office. But then, of course, he has plenty of time and inclination to serenade the pretty senoritas with his banjo."

"Was he a Don Juan?" I asked Dorothy's friend Carol Boyd. "He was not!" she replied. "He was always the gentleman. We took typing together. One day we were the only ones practising in the typing room. I stood up and my underskirt began to slip down. Percy saw it and said, 'Think nothing of it, Carol. Think nothing of it. I have three sisters. I'll just stand over here while you fix it.'" She laughed, "Margaret Thompson had a crush on him but he didn't have any special girl. He just liked us all."

Percy's class will also remarks on his musical talent and satirizes a junior who elsewhere in the yearbook is called "an all-round athlete": "Pike Stevens does will and bequeath his ability to chord in C on piano and banjo to Prunes Norcott, who will someday be a leader of a Hun-gary orchestra." Next to each senior's photograph is a literary quotation. Was Percy's selected by a spurned admirer? "He whistles as he goes, light-hearted wretch, / Cold and yet cheerful." (These verses, which refer to the postman, are from Cowper's "The Task," a poem popular in literature anthologies of the day. They are followed by a line that, in those early months of the war, was more truly prophetic than any in the *Pilot*: "Messenger of grief / Perhaps to thousands. . . .")

Guests invited to the Class of '17's graduation ceremonies were informed that commencement exercises would be held on Friday evening, 25 May, at eight o'clock, in the high school auditorium, that the Class motto was B² ("Be Square"—square, in those days, meaning just, fair, honest), the class flower the pink rose, and the class colors silver, gray, and pink. At the baccalaureate services Thursday night, the sermon was preached by W.C. Stewart of the Methodist Church, Percy's church. "We are living in a time when men's blood is being stirred as never before," the pastor told the seventeen seniors. "Humanity has been wronged, abused, outrageously mistreated.

America, true to her traditions of the past, could not sit idly by unmoved, but has, within a short time that has thrilled the world, responded to the appealing cry of the destitute and the forlorn. The cry has gone out over the hill and dale, sea and plain; young men are heeding the call of the country. A Great Service stretches out before you. You should thrill at the prospect."

E. P. Bolt, the popular young principal, awarded the honors and medals at the graduation ceremonies. The tennis doubles medal went to Percy and Arthur "Prunes" Norcott. Dorothy McCauley remembers Bolt: "He was a gifted teacher. When he came to the school it had been a pretty rough place. But he hadn't been there two or three months before he could go out of the room and come back and find it just as he had left it. He meant a lot to all of us. He was just the idol of the student body. He didn't qualify for the service; he had bad eyes. He died next year in the 'flu epidemic of 1918. He was only twenty-five."

"Doughboys" embarking for "regions unknown" at Hoboken, New Jersey.
(National Archives.)

OFF TO WAR

Six weeks before Percy's graduation the United States had declared war on Germany. Only one week before Percy received his diploma, Congress had passed the Selective Service Act, requiring all men between the ages of twenty-one and thirty to register for military service. Percy was not old enough to have to register but many of his friends were. One of them who signed up on "War Census Day" (declared a national holiday) was Frank Prince, his brother-in-law and my father; another was Rosewell P. Blake who, seven months later, would be Percy's cabin mate on the *Tuscania*. War fever was in the air, everywhere fanned by rhetoric like Pastor Stewart's, intensifying the pressure on those young men between eighteen and twenty-one to enlist, to heed "the call of the country," to respond to President Wilson's famous exhortation, made in April, to "make the world safe for democracy." One young soldier who survived the sinking of the *Tuscania* was to say later that seventy percent of the students at Oregon Agricultural College (now Oregon State University) had enlisted because "none of us wanted to be called a slacker." The press ran stories almost daily telling how humanity was being "wronged, abused, outrageously mistreated." This one appeared in the *Bend Bulletin* two weeks after Percy's graduation:

AMERICA MUST SAVE THE WORLD
"France is a graveyard and England is exhausted. America must save the world." That is the message brought ... today by William Humbleton from the battlefields of Europe.... The Germans take the dead from the fields, he declared today, to laboratories behind the lines where chemicals are made for gas bombs and certain kinds of shells and the acids used in gas attacks.

Even my father, whom I remember as the mildest of men, wrote to my mother from France a few months later: "The allies are taking fewer prisoners every battle. None would be still better ... the Hun must be absolutely exterminated and his country well fumigated before we leave."

In June 1917 America had been at war just two months and Percy was not yet eighteen. So he took a job as a stenographer with the Shevlin-Hixon

Author's father, Lt. Frank R. Prince, 1918.
(Author's collection.)

Lumber Company and on weekends and balmy summer evenings he played with his friends. "A jolly crowd of school students enjoyed a wiener roast on the banks of the river Wednesday evening," the *Bulletin* reported in July, naming Percy, Carol Boyd, and six others. "The crowd gathered round a large bonfire, music and wienie roasting making a general good time." The music could have been Percy's banjo. There were many evenings like that one, but as summer turned to fall, as more and more American troops were transported to France, the pressure on the "slackers" intensified. On 21 October the first "Sammies" (European nickname for American soldiers) had reached the front. More of Percy's classmates were enlisting.

Sometime that fall my father was commissioned a Lieutenant in the 20th Engineers and went off to Camp American University, Washington, D.C., leaving his wife at home with his young brother-in-law, his sister-in-law, his mother-in-law, and his two small sons.

Living at home with three women and two babies, reading stories such as Humbleton's, seeing his friends going off to war, Percy, not surprisingly, began to talk about enlisting. In August he turned eighteen, old enough to be accepted for military service, and in November he took the train up to Enderby to visit his father, most likely to get his approval. My father, by then in France, expressed in a letter to my mother what was probably the family's general reaction to Percy's plans: "I am wondering if Pike enlisted. I hope not, tho' there isn't much to say if he makes up his mind to do it." By December Percy had made up his mind.

Lt. Frank R. Prince and his French driver, "Somewhere in France," 1918.
(Author's collection.)

On the 12th he wrote from Portland to his mother that he and Rosewell Blake "couldn't get our exams today on account of the mob at the recruiting office." To pass the time they had gone to the Liberty Theater to see Bill Hart in "The Silent Man," and had heard a jazz orchestra at the Orpheum that "was just jake. Could hardly sit still." He also reported on the hazards of big-city life: "Last night Skinny was held up by two soldiers and robbed of his money, watch and cigarettes, so you bet the rest of us put our money in the hotel safe, so don't worry."

The next day he and Blake took the exams, passed, and were inducted into the army. On

Christmas Eve Percy wrote to his father: "Have just joined the U.S. Army in the 20th Engineers, Forestry Branch. Have been stationed at Vancouver [Washington] Barracks for about two weeks and am leaving for Washington, D.C., Wednesday morning. Will probably be in France in about two months." After asking how his father's new logging contract was coming, and joking about how his father had got "kind of fresh with a Ford," he concluded: "Well, Dad, it is now 12:35 so I think I'll quit and go to bed. It doesn't seem like Christmas a bit. This one won't be anything extra for you and myself, but believe me it's the last one we'll spend like this."

By 2 January, after a long, hard train ride, he was at Camp American University. He wrote that he had "pulled thru OK," but three soldiers who got sick on the train had been taken off at St. Louis. "What knocked them out was the grub, I guess: corned beef, bread, corned beef hash, hard tack, and coffee twice a day. Some food, hey?" All the Bend boys had been put into the same outfit, Company D of the 20th Engineers, "so it makes it jake." After a day or two of standing in line for equipment and shots, the rookies were given day passes.

While waiting to board a streetcar Percy and Blake had a serendipitous experience. They were joined by a civilian from Portland.

> So while we were talking a guy came up and asked us if we were in a hurry to get to town. We said yes, so he piled us into his seven passenger Packard. Well, we found out that this gink was the President of the Riggs National Bank in Washington, D.C. Some High Brow??? On the way downtown this Portland gink asked me how my money supply was. I said it was jake. He told us to let him know if we were broke. Just think. He told us to meet him at the Hotel Raleigh at 5:30, which we did. He ordered us dinner which consisted of chicken soup for me, Blue Point Oysters for himself and Blake, baked spuds, rice pudding, steak, breaded tomatoes, fried I guess, and some kind of salad. Then apple pie a la mode. It was the first good square dinner we had had since December 25 so you can imagine how good it tasted. Old Joe Cannon the big boy (Speaker of the House) sat at the table to our right! Gosh, he must be in his third childhood.

Cannon—"Uncle Joe"—the conservative congressman from Illinois, was then eighty-one—and he would live to be ninety—but he had not been speaker of the House since 1911.

Back at camp the boys heard a rumor they were going to be sent back to Oregon to work on spruce, then used for building airplanes, but Percy doubted it. He wrote that he had made the jazz band. "Play the drums. The banjo is busted. Have a great old time every night. The piano player is a gink out of our own company. In fact the whole bunch belong to Co. D. And say, is he a wonder. Plays just like Mrs. Horton. All the latest stuff out." The next day they again went into the city and walked until they were "just about dead."

They passed Billy Sunday's tabernacle. "The darn thing was just packed. The choir was singing their heads off. Am going to see and hear him."

Billy Sunday, the flamboyant, chauvinistic, evangelical preacher, was packing the public into his Tabernacle in spite of the tight-lipped disapproval of establishment critics. In October *Harpers* had printed an article in which a prominent psychologist had demonstrated that Sunday's actions were characteristic of one suffering from "infantilism." That same month the board of bishops of the Methodist Episcopal Church had gone on record deploring Sunday's "sensational evangelism." Two weeks before coming to Washington from Atlanta, Billy Sunday had made the headlines by engaging in fisticuffs on the platform of his tabernacle with a member of the audience who had objected to his comment, referring to the Germans, that he "didn't think God would be on the side of a dirty bunch that would stand aside and see a Turk outrage a woman." Observers agreed that the fight was a draw. A few days after Percy had walked past Sunday's hall, the Army arranged for his outfit to see this sensational showman. As Percy described the experience, with the satirical eye of a cartoonist, Billy Sunday did not disappoint the soldiers.

> Yesterday afternoon they took us out and drilled us for about three hours, and then we came back and washed up to go down and hear Bill Sunday. Well, we had special [street] cars to take us down to church first where they fed us two sandwiches and a cup

Billy Sunday (Portrait from *"Billy" Sunday: The Man and His Message* by William T. Ellis.)

of coffee. I went twice and got two doses. After grub the parade was formed and we were strung out for about four blocks long with civilians in the center. We marched down Pennsylvania Ave. to Bill's joint. Marched right in to reserved seats; gave a yell; then old Bill got up and started to speak after his choir of about 2,000 or 3,000 yelled a couple of pieces. He couldn't talk very loud on account of a cold, but we could hear most of it. First of all, he yanked off his collar, then stamped around, picked up a chair and slammed it down and sat in it. After running around the platform until he was winded he closed services. We then marched around and shook hands with the old boy, then went home on special cars. Believe me the old boy is some speaker.

On 18 January Percy wrote what was to be his last letter. "Dear Everybody: Well, here we are cooped up in the barracks waiting for the order to leave for some place or other. Maybe France—maybe some other camp; no one knows." He thanked them for "that dandy Xmas box. It sure was a peach. Just got the chance to open it the other day, and Blake and other Oregon ginks and myself just ate to beat the cars. Maybe those cup-cakes, fudge, raisins and everything didn't taste good. By gee, it was just like a big Xmas dinner!" The day before, he had taken out a $10,000 life insurance policy. "If I cast off then it will come in handy at home; if I get disabled for good, then I have it to live on. Worth more dead than alive. I made it out fifty-fifty between Ma and Pa." He concluded with a thoughtful reassurance: "If you should not hear for quite a while, don't get alarmed, because we may go to France, or we may go to any old place. The only sure thing is that we are to leave for regions unknown."

A few days later Percy boarded a train with the other members of companies D, E, and F, 20th Engineers, Forestry, and was taken to the port of embarkation at Hoboken, New Jersey. There these men, about 750, many from Oregon and Washington, joined seven other army units: aero squadrons 100, 158, and 213, made up of men from all over the country; four units of the 32nd Division, all from Wisconsin: the 107th Supply Train, the 107th Engineer Train, sanitary squads 7 and 8, and the 107th Military Police. All were under the command of Major Benjamin F. Wade. These troops, plus fifty-one "casual" (unassigned) officers and two civilians, making a total of 2,179 Americans, sailed with Percy Stevens on 25 January 1918 on the *Tuscania*.

THE TUSCANIA'S LAST VOYAGE

Nestled between the pages of my Grandmother's scrapbook, I found a post card of the *Tuscania*. By the standards of the great ships built in the thirties, such as the *Queen Elizabeth* (1938), the *Queen Mary* (1934), or the *Normandie* (1932), she looked small. But when the *Tuscania* was launched in September 1914, she was considered the finest of the Anchor Line's fleet of five ships. At 14,348 tons gross and nearly 550 feet in length, she was also the largest. Her twin-screws and four-gear turbine engines gave her a top speed of 15.5 knots. She could accommodate 2,417 passengers: 271 first class, 246 second class, and 1,900 tourist class. She could carry as many as fifty lifeboats.

The *Tuscania* had made her maiden voyage to New York in February 1915. In 1918, when Anchor Line leased her to Cunard Lines as a troopship, she was only three years old. Her commander for this voyage was an Anchor Line skipper, Captain Peter MacLean, fifty-one, from Glasgow. MacLean had been with Anchor Line for over twenty years and was a veteran of many Atlantic crossings. For his wartime services to King and Country he had just been awarded the Order of the British Empire. Two weeks later he was to remark wryly, "It's a funny thing, but the men they intend to decorate always seem to be torpedoed soon after." To the superstitious among the crew, the *Tuscania* had been living on borrowed time. She was the last of the Anchor Line's once proud Atlantic fleet. All four of her sister ships had been torpedoed within the last two years: the *Caledonia* in 1916; the *California* in February, the *Transylvania* in March, and the *Cameron* in April of 1917. Along with their captain, most of the crew of 235 were from Glasgow, many of them boys in their teens. There were two stewardesses.

The New England winter of 1917-18 was intensely cold. In January hundreds of homes ran out of furnace coal. They were relieved by ships of the Royal Navy that had smashed through the thick ice in Boston harbor to deliver coal not needed for bunkering their vessels in New York. When the *Tuscania* reached Halifax, Nova Scotia, the temperature was twenty degrees below zero and there were fears that she might be frozen in. But on

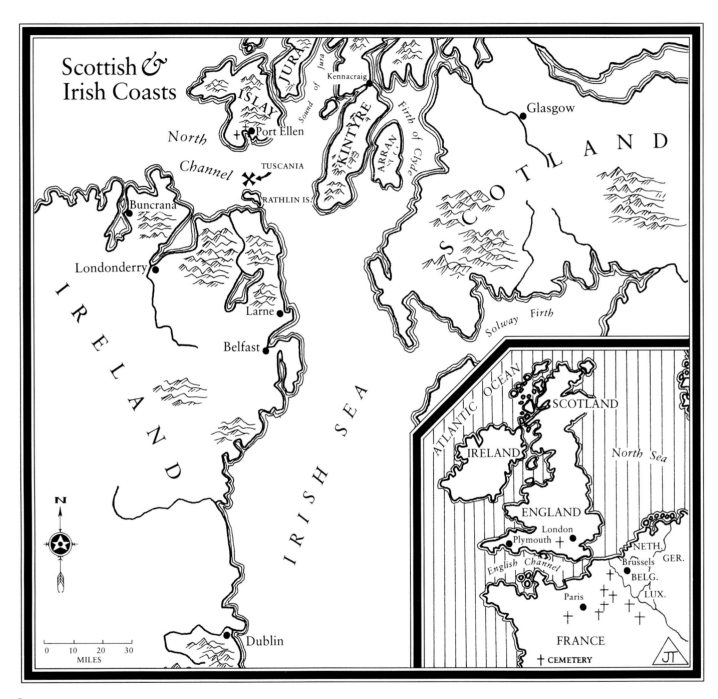

Scottish &
Irish Coasts

ISLAY
JURA
Sound of Jura
Kennacraig
KINTYRE
ARRAN
Firth of Clyde
Glasgow
North
Channel
Port Ellen
TUSCANIA
RATHLIN IS.
Buncrana
Londonderry
Larne
Belfast
S C O T L A N D
I R E L A N D
I R I S H   S E A
Solway Firth
N
0 10 20 30
MILES
Dublin

ATLANTIC OCEAN
SCOTLAND
IRELAND
ENGLAND
North Sea
London
Plymouth
NETH.
GER.
Brussels
BELG.
LUX.
English Channel
Paris
FRANCE
✝ CEMETERY
JT

18

The *Tuscania*, probably on her sea trials in 1914, soon after she was launched.
(National Archives.)

the afternoon of 27 January she managed to get out to the open sea. Once there she joined a convoy of ten other ships, all of them bound for England: three merchant ships, three cattle ships, two cargo ships, a collier, and another transport, the *Baltic*. All were escorted by the four-stacker cruiser, HMS *Cochrane*.

In 1925 Donald Smith, a survivor of the *Tuscania* voyage, described the first ten days of the "routine" crossing, "full of gossip and the usual wonderings as to whither bound, with the bar closed to us but leaking at times, with a make-believe boat drill, with the company clerks typing directives, with the old ivories working surrepti-

The *Tuscania* and the *Baltic* in convoy a few days before the *Tuscania* was torpedoed.
(From collection of Edward T. Lauer, Sr.)

tiously below into the small hours of the morning—in fact it was the same old crossing a couple million of us experienced." Another survivor of that voyage remembers the *Tuscania*'s cuisine: steamed potatoes without salt, fish, cheese, and "slum," a sort of stew whose ingredients, I suspect, are best left to the imagination. He recalled, too, that on the night before the torpedoing the soldiers had put on a concert at which one trooper with the requisite deep bass voice had given a moving rendition of "Asleep in the Deep."

On the eleventh day, the morning of 5 February, eight British destroyers had met the convoy and deployed themselves in front and on both sides of it. By late afternoon the flotilla of nineteen ships was off the northern tip of Ireland, about to enter the North Channel. The sky was overcast, the sea rough, with a steady wind blowing up from the south. At dusk, just after the conclusion of a boxing exhibition on deck, the soldiers began to get their first glimpses of land, Ireland on the right and Scotland on the left. Smith continues:

The sole topic of conversation was whether we were headed for Liverpool or Glasgow—but at least we were safe. Life belts which had been ten-day companions were quietly forgotten. We might see a little war after all.

I went on deck at about half past five and stood forward looking through a pitch black night at a light flashing three or four miles ahead. A figure appeared beside me.

"I wonder what that light is," I said.

"Rathlin Island," replied the figure. "Subs are bad here as they lie on the sandy bottom during the day and come to the surface when they hear us coming along." The speaker was the Second Officer about to go on watch.

I had never heard of Rathlin Island so I went into the smoking room where there was a big atlas, and succeeded in finding the spot—a little dot in the middle of where the Atlantic Ocean keeps the Scots and Irish apart. Just about there a ship had to decide whether she would head for Liverpool or Glasgow. The latest dope had it that we would be in Liverpool at seven o'clock next morning. This talk of a Bosch-infested sea must be all bosh.

While Smith was in the smoking room studying the atlas, another American soldier who had also seen the light on Rathlin Island was on deck talking to Patrick Cox, a young crew member. Their conversation was later reported in the *Glasgow Daily Record and Mail*:

"Well, are we out of the danger zone?" he asked.

"No," replied Cox. "We are still in the danger zone and may get a torpedo amidships at any moment."

The time was 5:45. For almost two hours the convoy had been stalked by a German submarine.

The U.B. 77, was one of the Kaiser's newest undersea warships. Although she was much slower than the *Tuscania*, with a speed of only 13.4 knots on the surface and 7.8 submerged, like all U-boats she had the same advantage over ships as a hunter over an elephant: a potent, sophisticated armament. Her five torpedo tubes were each loaded with a twenty-three-foot torpedo charged with 430 pounds of high explosives. One of these missiles traveling at a speed of twenty-eight knots could blow up a ship five miles away. The U.B. 77's crew of twenty-eight men and seven officers was commanded by Captain Wilhelm Meyer, age twenty-nine. In a letter he wrote in 1929 to the president of the *Tuscania* Survivors Association, Meyer said that the sinking of the *Tuscania* was "pure luck." The U.B. 77 had left Borkum, Germany, on 29 January, wrote Meyer, and

had been cruising off the northern Irish coast without once having to dive to save ourselves from attacks by British cruisers, which were supposed to be as thick as fish in that region.

Captain Wilhelm Meyer (center) and the officers and crew of U-boat 77. (Author's collection.)

U-boat 77, Captain Wilhelm Meyer and crew on deck. The caption (Eintaufen in die Schleuse
—diving into the lock) indicates that this photo was taken just after she was commissioned.
(Author's collection.)

Having given up hope of sighting prey in that area, I decided to head for the entrance to the North Channel, intending to enter the Irish Sea from the north.

Before going below, Meyer scanned the Atlantic for one last look.

With surprise and trembling I spotted an enormous cloud of black smoke on the west-ern horizon, heading directly toward me. I immediately ordered the U.B. 77 swung around and headed directly toward the smoke cloud, which was advancing south-easterly toward the Channel, evidently hav-ing taken the extreme north route across the Atlantic. Soon I was able to detect a huge seagoing caravan headed by a medium sized vessel, followed by a large white vessel with two smokestacks [this was the *Tuscania*], a large cruiser with four smokestacks and from six to eight smaller vessels. The whole caravan was flanked by what looked like myriads of destroyers.

The "medium sized vessel" was the other transport, the *Baltic*, actually a larger ship than the *Tuscania*. However, the *Tuscania* had been given a zebra appearance by the application of black zig-zag stripes on her white sides, and somehow this camouflage had created an illusion that caused Meyer to see her as larger than the *Baltic*.

I cruised above water back and forth in front of the advancing transports, trying to ascertain the chances of attack. I resolved to attack. I steered northeast. Dusk made visibility poor. There was constant danger we might underestimate the speed of the transports and be run down in their path. I had decided to attack without submerging. Suddenly, however, the destroyers pulled up all along the line, so that the leading destroyer was abreast of the transport. I thought I had been detected. We might easily have been seen because we were directly ahead of an advancing triple line consisting of a destroyer, a transport, and another destroyer. When there was no further sign that we had been detected, I decided to submerge. By that time darkness had fallen and sighting through the periscope was almost impossible. I had taken a good look at the largest transport before submerging but once we were beneath the water I could not find it through the periscope. My hands trembled as I moved the sighting apparatus because I knew that if I stayed much longer where we were the submarine would be rammed and sunk.

Meyer was not exaggerating. He was then only 1,200 meters—about three quarters of a mile—in front of the convoy, which was approaching him at a speed of twelve knots. It would be on top of him in less than three and a half minutes.

Suddenly, a vague, ghostly shadow crept across the sighting mirror. Then atop this shadow appeared the outline of a smokestack. I recognized this shadow as the largest transport. I immediately ordered two torpedoes fired.

Donald Smith was still in the smoking room. "What's the use of trying to describe what happened then? 'There was a loud report' would be perfectly good English, but it couldn't convey any description of the sound. The ship seemed to lift and shake; the lights went out, men pushed by in the dark hunting for the discarded life preservers and overcoats—something must have happened, but no one knew what it was. I dare say some of the survivors still think we struck a mine."

J. S. Peters, a crew member from Yorkshire who had already survived four torpedoings, two in the Mediterranean and two in the Atlantic, had come off watch at four o'clock and had gone on deck. "It was getting dark and there was a bit of fog on

The *Tuscania* in wartime "zebra" camouflage. (Artist unknown. From collection of Edward T. Lauer, Sr.)

the water. I got chatting with a trooper, and was showing him how to wear his life preserver, telling him how to put it always under his coat, so that he could get rid of it [the coat] dead easy if anything should happen. And the words were not right out of my mouth when the explosion came and the ship staggered."

Tom Smith, a boatswain's mate from Glasgow, was in the number one engine room chatting with a fellow boatswain when he heard "a terrific explosion and felt the boat heeling over. I said to my mate, 'They have got her now.'"

Donald Smith joined the crowd of soldiers groping their way in the dark down to their cabins two or three decks below.

Those men who had been carrying pocket searchlights deserve the reward for that night. When one is down below in a sinking ship the question of whether it were best to save the new thirty-five dollar boots, a tooth brush, or the socks Aunt Maud had just knitted for you does not arise. I did a little hurrying, forgot all the things I had made sure I would take in such an eventuality, and made the deck to find the complement of every boat drawn up where they were supposed to be. Mind you, I hadn't any position of command or particular responsibility in it so didn't have to hurry.

A Glasgow paper quoted "an American officer" on his troops' behavior just after the torpedo struck.

We were instantly disabled and all the lights went out. The order rang out, 'Troops to the boat stations, lifeboats out.' The shock was not severe—more of a crunching in feeling went through the ship than a direct blow. There was naturally at first a good deal of confusion; you cannot lower a score of lifeboats from an upper deck height in the darkness without some confusion, but at no time was there panic, though there was great excitement. This only lasted a few minutes, then everyone pulled himself together. Megaphone calls went over the ship: 'There is no danger of her sinking before all have been taken off.'

The British naturally acclaimed the "superb discipline and courage of the crew," as well as the "Troopers' Splendid Conduct." At home the *New York Times* under the headline, "Discipline the Salvation" proudly quoted a British officer's laconic tribute, "They were American soldiers." Still, there were some soldiers who, in those first minutes of excitement, donned their life preservers and jumped overboard, expecting to be picked up by the escorting vessels. Unfortunately the water temperature in the North Channel in February is about 47 degrees Fahrenheit. Those who were not picked up within two and a half hours, at the most, died of hypothermia.

John McMahon, a seventeen-year-old crewman, was on the port side when the torpedo hit on the starboard. "It was a terrific bang, and the whole ship shook; there was a lot of smoke also. All the lights went out and we took a strong list to starboard. There was no real panic. I heard soldiers in the first moments of darkness shouting, 'Keep cool, no rushing, you'll get there.'"

John McCanee, an engine room storekeeper, was one who needed no such admonition. McCanee had come on deck and was waiting to get into a lifeboat. Deciding that the *Tuscania* was in no imminent danger of sinking, he went back down into the bowels of the listing ship to his cabin where he retrieved six pounds fifteen shillings and some sticks of tobacco. With these safely stowed in his pockets he made his way back to the deck.

"All the lights went out," one of the soldiers remembered, "and I tried to make my way to my bunk to get my life preserver. The boat was beginning to list to starboard and men were running around shouting and tying on their life belts. I finally found mine and ran out on deck." Then he

Artist's impression of the scene just after the *Tuscania* was torpedoed. The destroyer *Pigeon* approaches the doomed ship from the side to take off soldiers. (From the *Sphere*, 16 February 1918. The Illustrated London News.)

describes a grotesque incident: "A Mexican came up beside me, looked overboard, stabbed himself and toppled over the rail into the water."

Donald Smith recalled, too, that the ship was in darkness for several minutes.

The Second Engineer who was on duty at the time, happened to be picked up by the same trawler as myself, and he told me that the explosion (which occurred on the starboard side in the stockhold 'midships) knocked

27

him off his feet as he stood at the controls. He made for the ladder but was up to his waist in water before reaching it, and on reaching deck helped to start the emergency dynamo, a gas engine on deck aft. With what I am going to say next two things must be remembered. First, the best men of the British Merchant Marine were all by that time in the Navy. The crew were anything that could be picked up in Liverpool or Glasgow. Second, our men were woodsmen, rather than sailors; the biggest unit was a battalion of the 20th Engineers. There is no need to dwell on the launching of the boats.... Each pair of davits was supposed to launch four boats—the average was possibly one each. In front of me as I stood at my station I saw a boat dropped from the top deck onto a loaded one in the water. I saw a loaded one held at one end and dropped at the other while soldiers tumbled out like ninepins.

The two stewardesses, the only women on board, were witnesses to one of these accidents, which happened just after they had descended a rope into a lifeboat already in the water. "The next boat tipped," said Mrs. Collins, "and immediately we were surrounded by men in icy cold water wearing life belts. We had only two men who could use the oars, but they did their best and as we came across swimming or floating men we gathered them in 'til the lifeboat was dangerously full." Mrs. Collins tried to save the life of one soldier whom they could not take into the crowded boat by holding on to his hands but he had died of

exposure before they were picked up by a destroyer four and a half hours later. Smith implied that if both crew and soldiers had been adept at lifeboat drill, more boats would have been launched. But the men were working in the dark on a wet, heaving, listing deck, a list that caused ropes to entangle and jam in pulleys. On the port side the list to starboard caused the boats to swing in and lodge against the side of the ship; on the starboard side they swung back and forth away from the hull, often out of reach of soldiers who plunged into the sea trying to leap into them.

Although they did not know it, the hundreds of men who were still waiting their turn to get into lifeboats were the lucky ones. They had not shared the fate of their shipmates who had had loaded boats fall on them, or who had been dumped out of tilting boats, or who had been killed in their boats when heavy inflatable life rafts had been tossed overboard and landed on top of them. And they would escape dangers that yet lay ahead for the ones already rowing away. All of them, like Donald Smith, wondered how long the *Tuscania* would stay afloat. Smith had been told that her sister ship, the *Transylvania*, had gone down in forty minutes after being torpedoed. Fifty minutes went by, an hour, two hours. Still the *Tuscania* floated. J.S. Peters, the four-times torpedoed crewman from Yorkshire, had a unique explanation: "And there was a very strange thing which I think accounted for the ship not sinking sooner. She went down about half past nine. One of the boats was lowered just where the torpedo had struck her, and the inrush of water carried the boat in and tightly wedged her there." (Another

Artist's impression of the destroyer *Pigeon* attempting to take soldiers off the sinking *Tuscania*. A lifeboat dangles from a davit and two soldiers who attempted to jump on to the *Pigeon*'s deck are falling into the sea. (From collection of Edward T. Lauer, Sr.)

crewman, using a simile that recalls this was still very much the day of the horse, reported that the hole in the hull was "as large as a carriage gateway.") A more prosaic explanation was given by the chief officer, R. W. Smart, who said that when the *Tuscania* was hit all the bulkhead doors had been tightly closed.

As crew and soldiers waited for lifeboats, some of them kept up their morale by singing. The crew sang "God Save the King," and the Americans—to the same tune, of course—"America." Another surviving crew member later reported that more lighthearted Yanks sang something like, "Oh! Oh! Where are we going from here?" This was the popular American Expeditionary Forces (AEF) song, "Slip a Pill to Kaiser Bill":

> Where do we go from here boys,
>   Where do we go from here?
> Slip a pill to Kaiser Bill
>   And make him shed a tear.
> And when we see the enemy
>   We'll shoot him in the rear.
> Oh, joy, Oh, boy, where do we
>   Go from here?

"All the while," wrote Smith, "we had been wondering what had become of our destroyer escort. Suddenly a light appeared and circled around us, finally becoming distinguishable as a destroyer, which came to rest bow to bow on the port side. Discipline relaxed a little, although not too much." Sergeant Archie E. Moore had been left in charge of his men while the officers were supervising the lowering of the lifeboats. In rec-

ommending Moore for the Distinguished Service Medal, his commanding officer described what it was like in those long minutes before the destroyers arrived.

About 8:00 P.M. all boats had been launched, and seemingly all means of escape were cut off. The ship was rapidly assuming a decided list to starboard which was becoming more and more acute. A smoke screen had been laid down by the destroyer which was convoying us at a distance of about fifty yards and it was impossible to see through this to note what attempts to rescue were being made. The statement "It's every man for himself now, men, take your chances," had been made in the hearing of the platoon by one of the officers. Sergeant Moore called the men to attention and for about an hour stood before them, keeping up their morale by talking to them—at first, when hope of rescue seemed good, by reminding them that their best chances lay in preserving perfect order and preventing all confusion. Toward 9:00 P.M. with the hope of final rescue becoming smaller and smaller, he told them that they were Americans and that their duty toward their country was, if their fate was to die, to die like Americans with a smile on their face and without fear. His words and his example kept those men, some of them less than four weeks out of civil life, at attention and in perfect order so that when the British destroyer *Pigeon* at last came alongside, they were able to march to the upper deck and get aboard the destroyer. (In spite of this commendation, Moore never got the Distinguished Service Medal.)

Part of the crew of the *Pigeon* were at mess on the lower deck when they clearly heard the rumble of a torpedo passing beneath their ship, a sound that must have stopped forks on the way to mouths. A few seconds later the *Tuscania* was hit, causing the *Pigeon*, which was on the port side of the troopship, to think that the attack had come from that quarter. Only when it was ascertained that the *Tuscania* had been struck on the starboard side did the *Pigeon*'s commander realize that the U-boat had fired two torpedoes, the first passing in front of the troopship and under the destroyer, the second finding its target. When the torpedo hit, the *Pigeon* and all of the other ships in the convoy kept right on going, "following orders, not desire," as one sailor later explained, so as not to present more targets to the submarine. Only when the convoy was considered to be safely away from the attacker were three destroyers, the *Pigeon*, the *Grasshopper*, and the *Mosquito*, ordered to return at full speed to the assistance of the stricken ship. The *Pigeon*'s petty officer, John N. Jones, recalled that on their run back they heard men in the water crying for help but could not see them in the dark, so his captain ordered him to lower the only boat, a "whaler," to search for survivors and to round up any lifeboats he came across, assuring him that he would return after the *Pigeon* had gone to the aid of the sinking ship. "Circumstances, however," wrote Jones, "caused a change in plan." The *Pigeon* was just pulling away from the *Tuscania*, after having taken aboard Sergeant Archie Moore and some eight hundred other men, when Meyer fired a third torpedo. It missed, but it was enough to make Jones's captain change his mind about sticking around to pick up his whaler. "For the sake of the 920 men or so that he had on board his ship," Jones explained, "he returned at full speed to his base," radioing to all ships in the vicinity to be on the lookout for his whaler. Jones rounded up eleven lifeboats and kept them together for several hours until finally he spotted a ship's lights, and with "an electric torch flashed a succession of Bs (----) which in the code means Boats." The rescuing vessel was the *Elf King*, one of several British trawlers fortunately in the North Channel that night. The fishermen hauled all the sailors and soldiers aboard—some 375 men—and took them safely to Larne, in northern Ireland.

Port nan Gallan Bay below Dun Athad, a mile east of the Mull of Oa. Several lifeboats were smashed on these jagged offshore reefs. See also photos on pp. 62 and 67 and the painting on p. 65. (Photo by Islay Shanks, Author's collection.)

TO REGIONS UNKNOWN

On board the *Tuscania* when the torpedo had struck, some men had been on deck, some in the smoking room, some at their respective posts. No doubt some had been below, working the "old ivories." One captain from Michigan told how he had just drawn a three of clubs to an inside straight; he never collected the pot. Some soldiers were at mess, others were preparing to go. Rosewell Blake was sleeping when Percy came to waken him for supper. Eleven days later, from "somewhere in England," Blake wrote to Grannie:

The lights went out instantly and the other men ran from the room. I jumped out of my bunk and got my life preserver in the corner where I had tied it. Percy called to me, "Blake, have you got my life preserver?" I told him I had not but to feel under the bunk and I would wait for him. He found it in a moment and we went out into the passageway and felt along the stairway. Percy while putting on his mackinaw dropped his preserver at my feet on the stairway. I picked it up and handed it to him and saw him put it on properly. He was assigned to a different boat and a different squad from mine. His boat was on the port side of the ship and mine was on the starboard side. When we reached the top of the main stairway we were separated to go to the ladder leading to the boat deck on our own respective sides. We had these boat drills every afternoon. Those were our orders and we were supposed to carry them out. Somehow I can never forgive myself for not violating those orders and keeping him with me. I have been reproaching myself constantly for ever letting him leave me. . . . I have talked to men who saw him on that side of the ship and they said he was cool and cheerful. They told me that when the officers called for men to go on the top deck and lift some lifeboats that had jammed, Percy was the first to go. My boat was the last to be lowered on my side of the ship and while waiting with my squad for a chance to lower it I went over to Percy's side looking for him. I called out to him and one of the men told me that he had got away safely with a number of others in the boat to which he had been assigned.

When U.B. 77's commander Meyer fired his torpedoes the nearest destroyer was less than five hundred feet away, and yet he was not spotted. He immediately dove to one hundred feet where he felt the shock waves of "a very violent explosion." When he came to the surface fifteen minutes later, the *Tuscania* had hoisted two white masthead lights and was sending out S O S radio signals. From these Meyer learned the name of his victim, which was listing to starboard and going down heavily by the stern. He submerged again to approach close before surfacing for another look but the sound of destroyers' propellers forced him to stay down. About half an hour later he again came up and found rescue operations fully underway. Determined to "hasten the steamer's sinking," he fired a third torpedo. But the poor visibility led Meyer to think that the *Tuscania* was moving forward at a speed of two knots when she was actually dead in the water, so his shot, which he had aimed ahead of the ship, passed harmlessly across her bow. This attack caused the *Pigeon*, already heavily loaded with soldiers, to suspend rescue operations and head for Ireland. But the *Mosquito* charged off and dropped depth bombs, an action which started a rumor that the U-boat had been sunk, a rumor converted into hopeful conjecture in most of the British press, including the *London Times*, and into exultant fact in the headlines of the *Glasgow Evening News*: "U-Boat Bombed / Tuscania's Assailant Sunk."

The submarine was not sunk, of course. At the Armistice, Captain Meyer surrendered her at the English east coast port of Harwich. She was later broken up and sold for scrap. But as Donald Smith so well expressed it, "A couple thousand of us wanted that submarine sunk." Meyer's report that he had surfaced to fire a third torpedo makes possible, if not plausible, a story told by the *Tuscania*'s second officer, G.K. Lynas, who had been in a lifeboat with forty others: "All at once we bumped into something hard, and when I looked 'round, here's the submarine lying awash—up to see what dirty work had been done." Asked by open-mouthed reporters what they did next, Lynas blandly replied, "What did we do? What could we do? We simply carried on. And soon we were picked up."

Some Scottish newspapers printed a report from a "North of Ireland correspondent" that the *Tuscania* had sunk while an attempt was being made to tow her for beaching on the Irish coast. But when Captain Meyer surveyed the scene once again at 9:00 P.M. he wrote in his log, "Nothing more can be seen of the ship. A number of destroyers are steaming about. Morse signals everywhere. Nothing to be seen of any vessel in tow. I assume that she has foundered." Two eyewitnesses gave reporters differing versions of the ship's last moments. Patrick Wilkinson, an American from a "university in New Hampshire" had sat in a leaking lifeboat in water up to his waist for six hours before being picked up. Not surprisingly, he could only speak in a "hoarse whisper," but he gave a colorful account: "her bow dipped, there was a series of explosions, great blasts of flame shot from her stacks, and she disappeared." The young crew member, Patrick Cox, saw the ship's end from another lifeboat: "The liner went down nose first, and when in an upright position suddenly overturned." Fifteen years later another soldier remembered the scene quite differently: "I watched her go down, gently it seemed to me, without any explosion, buckling or breaking in two, which some report—and as she went down a gentle glow was seen in the shape of a bowl over the spot where she sank."

Cox and Wilkinson had been in two of a number of lifeboats whose occupants were picked up by the destroyers and trawlers and taken to three Irish ports, Buncrana on Lough Swilly, Londonderry on Lough Foyle and Larne, north of Belfast. Captain MacLean, wearing full uniform under his oilskins, was landed at Glasgow with eighty survivors. He refused to be interviewed. Major Benjamin Wade, the commander of the American troops, was taken from Larne to Belfast with 546 of his soldiers. While dining with some of them he was handed a message of sympathy from the Town Council. He "broke down and sobbed like a child for several minutes."

There was joy in Belfast, too, as the *London Times* reported.

More than 100 American soldiers, survivors of the Tuscania, arrived in Belfast yesterday, and were escorted to temporary headquarters by a band of the Royal Irish Rifles. The men had an enthusiastic reception at the railway station, and their march through the streets aroused considerable enthusiasm.

The townspeople provided the men with comforts and luxuries, and a smoking concert was given in the Town Hall, at which several of the soldiers contributed musical items. The female employees in a local works collected among themselves sufficient money to provide each man with a considerable quantity of cigarettes.

These were the fortunate ones. Percy and the others who had not been picked up had no choice as to which direction they would go to find land. The strong wind and the powerful prevailing current in the North Channel, each coming out of the south, combined to drive their boats inexorably northward directly toward the southern end of the Hebridean island of Islay and to the fist-like peninsula called the Oa. Here the black, shaley cliffs rise four hundred feet sheer out of the Atlantic to the promontory known as the Mull of Oa. A mile to the east is craggy Dun Athad. Between these two heights is lonely Port nan Gallan bay, its entrance guarded by a half mile of jagged reefs and innumerable rocky islets. As midnight approached, the wind picked up and the sea became rougher. The lifeboats, rising and falling on the heavy swells, approached the Oa. Arthur Siplon, a member of the 100th Aero Squadron, was in one of them. In his vivid account, in which he describes the stormy night, we live what must have been Percy's last few moments before he left "for regions unknown":

As the hours went by, the intensity of the storm increased. We could not control the

35

Robert Morrison (pointing) and John Woodrow, on wrecked *Tuscania* lifeboats. Morrison is pointing to the cliffs of the Mull of Oa from which he and Woodrow rescued several American soldiers. (National Archives.)

boat, and it was caught sideways in the trough of the waves, and pitched from crest to crest. Midnight came without relief, and one man who was ailing died of exposure. During the early hours of the morning a cry went up, "A big wave is approaching!" We strained our eyes and found, off in the distance, land could dimly be made out. Soon we could hear faintly the roar of the roll of heavy surf. Shortly it became louder, sounding a threat of imminent disaster. Still moving sideways in the trough of the waves, we were suddenly caught with a mighty heave and sent crashing into the boiling angry sea. As I reached the surface, the boat was bottom side up in front of me. I could hear men screaming and praying all about me. With great effort I scrambled up on the bottom of the boat. My closest pal, Wilbur Clark, of Jackson, Michigan, came up near me. He, too, reached a place on the boat; we were the only ones able to make it. But in just a brief moment a big wave drove us off into the raging sea again. It was then a matter of being buffeted from rock to rock, washed in with the waves and out with the undertow. When it seemed my last breath was reached, when the next one would be the final one, I was struck forcibly in the chest. I grabbed with both hands. As the next wave went out I found I was on the point of a rock near the shore. I gripped with all my strength and tried to recover my breath. As the next wave went out a dark object was thrown up near me. It was another survivor; he was alive, for I could hear him faintly offering a prayer. He could hardly move, but I got him up, placing him on a rock with me. Though I was badly battered, two big cuts on my head, my body bleeding in many places, my mind remained alert. Thinking that the tide might rise, I placed the arms of the boy over the rock to hold him on, and then scrambled on my hands and knees toward the solid wall of rock that appeared to be the shoreline. Crawling about I found a big crevice in the rock. I moved into it and rose above the water line.

Having found this sanctuary, Siplon returned to the boy on the rock and slowly and painfully brought him to the cave. Here they "snuggled up in each other's arms like a couple of bear cubs in

Jetty Shanks at about 26. She sheltered several *Tuscania* survivors the night of the torpedoing. See the photo of her house on p. 39. (Author's collection.)

an effort to keep from freezing to death." When dawn broke, they saw many bodies bobbing around in the shallows. One of them was Siplon's pal, Wilbur Clark. Another was Roy Muncaster, a forest ranger from Washington's Olympic Peninsula. He and his buddy, Sergeant Everett√ Harpham, had been tossed out of the boat into the surf. As they both clung to a rock Muncaster√ yelled, "Cheer up, Harp, we'll get the Kaiser yet." A wave swept Harpham to safety, Roy Muncaster drowned. The fortunate few, like Harpham and Siplon, who had been thrown up at the base of the Oa might have perished there but for the efforts of two "Coast Watchers," farmers who lived near the cliffs whose duty it was to be on the lookout for shipwrecked sailors. Siplon and the boy were found by Robert Morrison who had been alerted by four survivors when they found his cottage after scaling the cliffs. Morrison rescued three men who were marooned on a rock by wading out up to his neck and tossing them a rope, then he climbed 250 feet up the cliff to the aid of an injured soldier who had got stuck on a ledge trying to reach the summit, and carried him on his back to safety. The second coast watcher, Duncan Campbell, went down to the rocky shore at 3:00 A.M. and brought groups of soaked and injured men to his tiny cottage. There his sister, Annie, built a blazing fire and began baking "girdle scones." When the butter ran out her sister churned some more and Annie kept on baking. By eight o'clock when her supplies finally were exhausted she had served her scones to nearly one hundred men, all of whom, if asked, would have agreed she deserved a medal for her baking that night. But four months later it was her brother and Morrison who were awarded the Order of the British Empire.

Not all of the boats were wrecked on the rocks; some made it to shore without so much as a scraped bottom. On Islay, people still tell of the lifeboat in which one of the crew was a native son, an electrician named Ronnie MacDonald. When his boat neared the island, MacDonald ordered the rowers to back off and hold position offshore until dawn. The story goes that when some of the seasick and shivering men demanded that Mac-Donald take them into port, he pulled out a pistol and held them off. At daybreak he guided the lifeboat around the rocks and safely into the harbor.

Another boat, by whimsical chance, was swept past reefs, rocks, and cliffs, straight into Port Ellen harbor. The soldiers were taken in that night by the local school teacher, Jetty Shanks, and her sister Bella. Later that year, three months before the Armistice, Jetty wrote about that memorable night to the mother of Ed Brownell, one of her unexpected guests:

It was my privilege to entertain seven of the survivors of the ill-fated Tuscania, and among them your son. Your son says that possibly you might like me to tell you about that time. The transport was torpedoed about eighteen miles from Islay on the Tuesday or Monday evening and the survivors arrived in boats early the next morning. The sea was very rough, and evidently the boys knew little or nothing of the handling of boats, and in such an angry sea the results were disastrous. Our coast is very rocky. The difficulty of ascending the cliffs, in their exhausted condition, was awful, many perished, being dashed against the rocks. Your son, if I am right, and I think now that I am,

85 Frederick Crescent of Port Ellen, Islay, where Jetty Shanks sheltered some of the *Tuscania* survivors the night of 5 February 1918. See Jetty's photo on p. 37. (Author's collection.)

had to cut off the sleeves of his shirt to tie himself to his lifeboat. He had lost everything, his greatcoat and other coat, and had contracted a very bad cold. Having plenty of room, we had seven of them, put on rousing fires and had quite a nice evening. My sister had some liniment in and she doctored your son and he was able to join in the singing, etc., we had after dinner. I remember him singing, "Mother's Rosary."

For days the bodies washed ashore, Jetty wrote, until, in the little plot at Kilnaughton, across the bay from Port Ellen, there were nearly 180 graves. She told how, on the way to her school, she would pass little groups of women, "weeping as for their own." And, obviously worried that Mrs. Brownell would think she had a romantic interest in her son Ed, Jetty hastened to assure her that her "dancing days" were long since past (she was then forty-eight), that she wrote only as a friend. "I have a little nephew called Islay," she concluded, "all [else] that I hold dear is lying beneath the green sod, but still we must go on."

Rescue operations had begun the moment the *Tuscania* was hit. They went on throughout the night of 5 February and continued the following day. Because survivors were landing in at least five widely separated places—Islay, three ports in Ireland, and Glasgow—the tasks of counting and listing both survivors and casualties was complicated and confusing. Perhaps this explains why General Pershing's cable from his headquarters in France informing Secretary of War Newton Baker of the sinking did not reach Washington until late in the afternoon of 6 February, more than twenty-four hours after the event. It *is* the reason why Baker waited several more hours before making the news public. His dilemma was melodramatically recreated in an article, "A Piece of Paper," in the May 1918 issue of *Good Housekeeping* magazine. The author, David Wilhelm, imagines the dialogue that took place late Wednesday afternoon between Baker and the War Department's chief censor, Major General Frank McIntyre, as they looked at Pershing's cable:

The eyes of the two men were resting on the piece of paper that lay there, like a thing of personality, on the glass that rests above colored maps of the old, the embattled world. At last the Secretary spoke.

"General," he said, setting his jaw forward, "I can't help thinking of all those families—"

The General nodded. "I know, Mr. Secretary," he said, simply.

"It may be," the Secretary resumed, "that many of the men on the transport are being saved. And there are so many units represented—"

There was a tense little pause.

"General, we shall wait for confirmation."

Then another pause. Yet the two stood there, eyes intent on that little piece of paper.

That was all. A few dots and dashes, symbols for sinister words unknown, had recorded the loss of a thousand men, it seemed. A hand—a grim hand, a harsh, malignant, and merciless hand—had reached up through the bottom of that great ship and closed its tight fingers on more than a thousand lives—American lives!

The Secretary repeated, "We shall wait for confirmation, General."

The General, in whose keeping are the lists of soldiers' loved ones, nodded approval.

The Secretary waited. One hour! Another! He hastened home for a few moments with his family, then back.

The General waited in his office before the two windows that front on Pennsylvania Avenue.

The great building itself waited, looming smaller, somehow, there beneath the great arch of the darkening sky. . . .

At last, at 9:15, one of the telegraphers of the Navy took a message of a hundred words. It meant nothing whatever to him.

He put it on the automatic carrier. It sped over the court to the Communications Officer. He passed it on to the decoders. An ensign and a yeoman deciphered it. In fifteen minutes copies of it were on the way to the Chief of Naval Operations, to the two Secretaries, and to the aides of the President.

Ralph Hayes, Secretary Baker's private secretary, notified the Committee on Public Information. Its night editor called in the newspaper man. Soon a million telegraphic dots and dashes were bounding away, leaping telltale to the world. And soon in all the great cities, extras were being shouted. Mothers and fathers, sleeping, heard and wakened. Fear gripped their hearts. Strong men clenched their fists, weak ones cried.

Mars at last had crossed the sea, invaded America's very homes, taken deliberately her chosen sons.

When Baker finally released the news to the press, President Wilson was at Keith's Theater with Mrs. Wilson and her brother and sister-in-law, Mr. and Mrs. Joseph Bolling, enjoying a vaudeville show. Wilson did not hear of the sinking of the troop ship until he returned to the White House around midnight nearly thirty-six hours after U. B. 77's torpedo had slammed into the *Tuscania*'s hull.

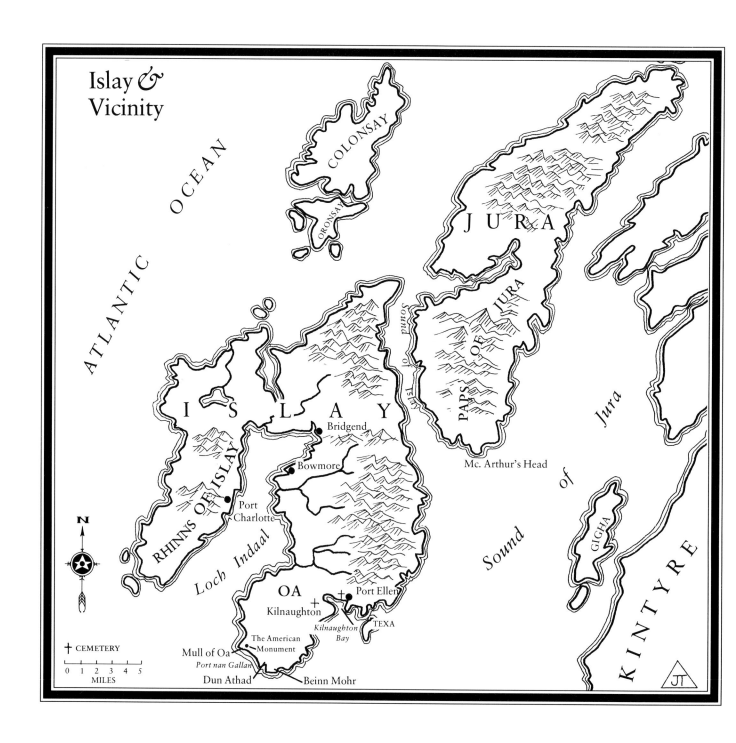

Islay & Vicinity

ATLANTIC OCEAN

COLONSAY

ORONSAY

JURA

PAPS OF JURA

Sound of Jura

ISLAY

Bridgend

Bowmore

RHINNS OF ISLAY

Port Charlotte

Mc. Arthur's Head

Sound of Islay

GIGHA

Loch Indaal

OA

Kilnaughton

Kilnaughton Bay

Port Ellen

TEXA

The American Monument

Mull of Oa

Port nan Gallan

Dun Athad

Beinn Mohr

N

+ CEMETERY

0 1 2 3 4 5
MILES

KINTYRE

JT

REMEMBER
THE TUSCANIA

The sinking of the *Tuscania* made the front page of every newpaper in the country. American soldiers had already died in the war and American ships had been sunk, but the *Tuscania* was the first troopship to be torpedoed. The *Antilles* had been sunk with a loss of fourteen lives in October 1917, but she was on her return voyage. The sinking of the *Tuscania*, like no other event since the declaration of war, shocked Americans into realizing that Mars had indeed "crossed the sea." By Thursday morning, 7 February 1918, over forty-eight hours had elapsed since the sinking, and over twelve hours since Pershing had sent his cable, so that when newspapers did hit the streets the accounts were remarkably accurate. The *New York Times* carried a banner headline: "TUSCANIA CARRYING 2,179 U.S. TROOPS SUNK / 1,912 SURVIVORS LANDED AT IRISH PORTS / WASHINGTON FEARS 260 MEN ARE LOST." Below the headline is a three-column photograph of the ship and a list of units aboard. The story stayed on the front page for a week.

The daily *Bend Bulletin* was an afternoon paper. Under this headline, "FIRST OF AMERICAN TRANSPORTS IS TORPEDOED," it printed a hopeful conjecture obtained from Grannie that morning: "From Percy Stevens a card was received Sunday night apprising [his mother] of his sailing but not mentioning what boat he would be on. It may be possible that he had already arrived in France on one of the other boats as a large number of boats are known to be crossing this week." On Friday the *Bulletin* printed the names of the five Bend boys who were on the transport and, also on the front page, inside a black border, this "Special Report": "Mrs. Frank Prince just received a cablegram that her brother, Percy Stevens, and Roscoe [Rosewell] Blake are among the survivors of the Tuscania." The message had been sent by "Judge Blake of New York City," Rosewell Blake's father. The euphoria created by Judge Blake's message carried Grannie and her daughters through the weekend, but Monday's news brought an abrupt letdown. The *Bulletin* reported that two Bend boys, George Shafer and Edward Peterman, were safe, but that thirty-two

Oregon soldiers were missing, including Percy A. "Stephens." The next day the *Times* printed a complete list of the 347 missing. Percy's name was on it, now spelled correctly. By this time both Percy's father in Enderby and his brother-in-law's father in St. Paul had been telephoning the War Department trying to determine Percy's true fate. On Wednesday, Saint Valentine's Day, they learned it. Early that cold morning Percy's mother and sisters received the news (made all the more bitter after they had lived for five days on the hope given them by Judge Blake's telegram) that their son and brother had been buried on "the coast of Scotland." The same day the *Oregonian* printed a list of "79 buried side by side" in Scotland. Number thirty-nine was Percy A. Stevens.

Why did Judge Blake send the telegram? The mistake must have originated with Rosewell. He had been told just before he got into his lifeboat that Percy "had got away safely with a number of others in the boat to which he had been assigned." Assuming that Percy had landed safely someplace, he must have cabled his father that message.

Islay, the "coast" where Percy was buried, is a small island twenty-eight miles long from north to south and about twenty miles across at its widest point. From the south Loch Indaal cuts deeply up into the center of the island, separating the western peninsula, the Rhinns of Islay, from the Oa. Since the main centers of population, the villages of Port Ellen, Bowmore, Bridgend, and Port Charlotte, are all situated on the tortuous southern coastline where both survivors and victims were washed up, practically everyone on Islay was touched by the tragedy, from the school teacher

Jetty Shanks at Port Ellen to the Laird of Islay, Hugh Morrison, at Islay House near Bridgend. It was Morrison who ordered trees cut from his estate to provide wood for the coffins and who gave land for two of the four burial grounds where the dead were first interred.

On the day before the first of several funeral services, the islanders discovered that there was no American flag available for the ceremony, so Mary Armour, Florence Hall, Jessie McClellan, Catherine MacGregor and John McDougall worked through the night sewing one, using as a model a wallet-sized flag given them by a soldier. On 13 February an honor guard of soldiers, and a cortege of islanders led by a piper playing a lament, marched the mile from Port Ellen around the circuit of the shore to the grassy slope above the beach at Kilnaughton Bay. The ceremony they performed here for Percy and the seventy-eight soldiers buried beside him was photographed by Archibald Cameron, an enterprising bookseller and printer from Bowmore. Cameron quickly got out a "Souvenir Album of the Tuscania Disaster, 5th February, 1918, And Burial of American Soldiers in Islay." His photo shows the honor guard of black-suited men of Islay firing a salute over the mounded, flower-covered graves. Beside the piper stands an islander holding the Union Jack while a soldier holds the homemade Stars and Stripes. This flag, measuring thirty-six inches by sixty-nine inches, was displayed at all of the funerals for the *Tuscania* dead after which Hugh Morrison presented it to Associated Press correspondent Frank M. America, the first American reporter to reach Islay after the disaster. America gave it to

A funeral procession leaving Port Charlotte in the rain, passing the distillery which was made into an improvised morgue. Pipers lead the cortege. American soldiers, survivors from the *Tuscania*, escort the one motor lorry and the three wagons carrying the coffins. A crowd of mourners follow. (National Archives.)

Mary Armour, Florence Hall, Jessie McClellan, Catherine McGregor and John McDougall, the five who made the American flag for the funerals of the *Tuscania* victims. See photos on pp. 49 and 67. (Smithsonian Institution.)

President Wilson who put it in the Smithsonian Institution. It is housed today in the Smithsonian's Museum of American History.

Back in Percy's home town, the *Bend Bulletin* informed the community of his death: "First Bend Boy Killed in War." Flags were flown at half mast all over the city. The weekly Hippodrome dance was cancelled and a card party to have been held at the Emblem Club was called off. The Bend Commercial Club sent a message to Percy's mother and sisters expressing its "deepest sympathy and condolences," assuring them that "you will also feel proud that you have given the supreme sacrifice, in the gift of Percy Stevens, in the universal cause of Liberty." It congratulated them "on the patriotic sacrifice you have made in giving the life of him who died in the defense of you and our homes and humanity." Two days later the Shevlin-Hixon office staff presented to them the gold star. The student body of Bend High School held a special service. Later they gave the school a memorial to their schoolmate, a painting of Sir Galahad, the purest and finest of King Arthur's Knights of the Round Table.

From Washington, Secretary of War Newton Baker issued a statement that was quoted with satisfaction in both the national press and in Britain: "The sinking of the Tuscania brings us face to face with the losses of war in its most relentless form. It is a fresh challenge to the civilized world by an adversary who has refined and made more deadly the stealth of the savage in wartime. We must win this war and we will win this war."

From New York to Bend, Baker's theme that the war was a crusade against "the savage" was echoed with varying degrees of rancor. Hearst's *New York American* announced that "the nation is aroused, and angry. We are going to beat Germany if it takes any number of years and all the blood and wealth we have to spend. The sinking of the Tuscania has bound up all American hearts in the firm resolve to fight to a finish against German frightfulness." At a memorial service in New York where messages were read from Governor Charles S. Whitman, Cardinal Gibbons, Thomas Edison, and ex-President Taft, several clergymen, while admitting that the sinking was a barbarous act on the part of the German war machine, tried to make the point that most persons of German stock in the United States were good Americans. Municipal Court Justice Blake, Rosewell's father, violently disagreed:

> The preachers have told us that Germans here are red-blooded Americans. I have reason to know that that is false. The German people are back of the blasphemous and sacrilegious Hun who heads their government. I tell you it is time the American people took on a spirit of revenge, and I hope that for every one of those scarred bodies thrown up on the Irish [*sic*] coast a thousand Huns shall fall. For the barbarity of the Huns let us return in measure a thousand fold.

The day after the news broke, the *New York Times* carried a full-page Treasury Department ad urging the purchase of "Thrift Stamps" at a quarter each. There is a sketch of a sinking transport, lifeboats and men in the water, the conning tower

Oregonian cartoon, 9 February 1918.

of a U-boat. "What will be *your* answer? The *Tuscania* lies at the bottom of the ocean, a victim of German ruthlessness. With her are some of our boys who have given their lives that you and I here at home may be safe." In Chicago, Bainbridge Colby, a member of the United States Shipping Board, told the members of the Iroquois Club that submarine warfare "is not war. It is a demon thing conceived in the degenerate mind of a ghoul." In Portland, the *Oregonian* featured on the front page a cartoon: a ship is sinking in a dark, stormy sea. Lifeboats are in the water, one dangles from

Fourth of July celebration 1918 in front of the Liberty Theater in Bend, Oregon. Ward H. Cable, the author's uncle and the owner of the theatre, is standing between two nurses. (Author's collection.)

the davits. Out of the waves rises an arm labeled "Kultur." Its mailed fist holds a dagger labeled "Murder." In Bend the *Bulletin* carried an ad for the Liberty Theater's current offering, Ira M. Lowry's "For the Freedom of the World," a film it called "the greatest spectacle ever conceived." Moviegoers are promised "a realistic reproduction of the life of your sons, fathers and brothers . . . and the hardships they will later be privileged to undergo in the trenches. . . . What is the price," asks the Liberty management, "of American boys—Your Own Boys—of the *Tuscania*? See 'For the Freedom of the World,' Nights 15 cents–35 cents." Parents are urged to send their children to the matinees (10–20 cents): "It will teach them patriotism."

The theme that the soldiers had died both for their country and in the cause of humanity was also sounded by the poets. "A.W." (the Irish poet George Russell) wrote in the *Literary Digest* that "The Tuscania Dead" had been "Robbed of their part on Europe's epic stage,"

> Yet on their breasts a heaven of stars I see,
> All that a noble cause bequeaths is there,
> Above their tomb new western chivalry
> Rides to fulfill their prayer.

In *Scribner's Magazine*, Mary Raymond Shipman Andrews chose Whitmanesque verse to exhort her countrymen in "A Call to Arms." The first stanza of her work is in the adjacent column.

The official American toll from the sinking was finally fixed at 230. In March, Representative James of Michigan introduced a bill to return the 171 bodies buried on Islay to Arlington National Cemetery. Four months later the American Red Cross announced plans to construct a monument on the Mull of Oa. Unfortunately before action was taken on either proposal the rocky shores of Islay were once again strewn with the bodies of American soldiers. In October the British merchant cruiser *Otranto*, carrying American troops, was accidentally rammed by the *Kashmir*, another ship in her convoy in almost the same place where the *Tuscania* had gone down eight months before. Unlike the *Tuscania*, the *Otranto* sank almost immediately with the result that 356 soldiers drowned. For a second time that year the people of Islay had to build coffins and dig graves. They found and buried 241 men alongside the *Tuscania* dead.

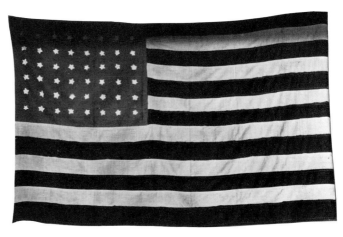

The stars and stripes made by the five inhabitants of Islay and used at the funerals for the *Tuscania* dead. See the photo on p. 57. (Smithsonian Institution.)

It is I, America, calling!
Above the sound of rivers falling,
Above the whir of wheels and the chime of bells
  in the steeple
—Wheels, rolling gold into the palms of the
  people—
Bells ringing silverly clear and slow
To church-going, leisurely steps on pavements
  below.
Above all familiar sounds of the life of a nation
  I shout to you a name.
And the flame of that name is sped
Like fire into hearts where blood runs red—
The hearts of the land burn hot to the land's
  salvation
As I call across the long miles, as I, America,
  call to my nation!
Tuscania! *Tuscania*!
Americans, remember the *Tuscania*!

Kilnaughton Bay, looking toward the lighthouse. This is the scene A. Shanks painted from memory. (Author's collection.)

THE TUSCANIA'S LEGACY

Sunday, 11 May 1980, Mother's Day. My wife Joan and I take the bus from Glasgow to Kennacraig and board the red and white Mac-Brayne's auto ferry, *Iona*, bound for Islay. Up here on deck a brisk breeze blows in our faces as the ship plows a white furrow down West Loch Tarbert. A nervous German shepherd, an alien and a landlubber, whimpering uneasily, huddles next to his master. Two perky Scottish terriers, thoroughly enjoying the voyage, lead their mistress at a sprightly pace around the deck. On our left rise the soft, felt-green hills of Kintyre, dotted with white dairy cows. To the right the land is all brown heather and gray, rocky outcroppings. It is as if the loch were a blue margin separating the Lowlands from the Highlands. At the mouth of the loch the *Iona* steers due south, then turns southwest, passing close by the tiny island of Gigha on the port side. Back from its rocky shore Gigha is softly mounded, green, and grassy. A group of white buildings snuggle in a hollow, one of them the familiar Highland farmhouse with gabled ends and twin chimneys. Out of the soft haze to our right slowly materialize the Paps of Jura:

Beinn a Chaolais, 2407 feet; Beinn Shiantaidh, 2477 feet; Beinn an Oir, 2571 feet. Now we turn west, past a rocky chunk of an islet where a fat seal dozes and eider ducks stare. Out of the haze, like images on a developing photograph, the hills of Islay form on the horizon. Soon we can see the black brow of the promontory Mc.Arthur's Head guarding the sound separating Islay from Jura. Ahead, almost due west, the southern tip of Islay lies half submerged on the horizon, like the head and jaws of a sleeping crocodile. This is the Oa. I study the Oa with my binoculars as I try to focus on a cold February night over sixty years ago. There, against these sheer cliffs the *Tuscania*'s lifeboats were smashed. There, or near there, Percy died. We search for the monument that the American Red Cross built in 1920, but it is on the western side, hidden from us by the great bluff of Rubha nan Leacan.

The *Iona* shudders and swings sharply to starboard, rounding the offshore island of Texa, heading north for Port Ellen. Approaching the harbor we can see on our left a white blocky building. I recognize it as the "tower" in the painting done by "A. Shanks," a copy of which was in my

The White Hart Hotel at Port Ellen, Islay. Used as a first aide station for the survivors of the *Tuscania* disaster. (Author's collection.)

childhood room. It is a lighthouse. Just beyond it on the green slopes above the beach rise the stones and monuments of the old cemetery. Somewhere is the plot where Percy was buried. Most of Port Ellen—stone houses, slate roofs, twin chimneys, all white except for black, green, or red window and door trim—lies off to the right of the pier.

On the dock we carry our suitcases past the open door of MacBrayne's booking office. Inside, a young woman is carrying on a lively telephone conversation in Gaelic. We pass the red pillar box of H.M. Post Office, the blue and white Lloyds Bank, turn the corner and go down the narrow street past the Trout Fly pub to the White Hart Hotel, white with black trim, four dormer windows on the third story facing the bay. The hotel was used that night in 1918 as a temporary hospital. Here the first islander to greet us is tubby Sheba, the hotel's resident black labrador. A young man takes us up to a sunny room with a view. Out one of the dormer windows we look west across the bay to Kilnaughton churchyard.

It is still early afternoon, so we put on our hiking boots and set out along the arc of Port Ellen harbor, past the whisky distillery (founded in 1827, one of eight still operating on the island) from which we get a seductive whiff of "Islay Single Malt," then down a narrow, blacktop lane bordered by neat stone walls, nicely laid up dry, the horizontal flat rocks capped at four feet by a course of rocks set vertically and fixed with mortar. Primroses bloom along the base of the walls. Bluebells wave beyond them. We turn down a footpath and cross a pasture. Placid ewes nibble the short grass. Skittery spring lambs bound away, bleating. We walk along the golden beach, then climb up the low dunes and onto the green slopes. In front of us four low stone walls enclose a square sixty feet on a side—this is the x on the painting. Within are eleven gravestones, six in a row along the west wall. We push the rusty iron gate and enter. On the first stone the name *Tuscania* jumps out at me. Joan reads the inscription: "'Trimmer, J. Logan, s.s. Tuscania, 5th February 1918.' What's a trimmer?"

"He shoveled coal from bunker to bunker to keep them balanced. He trimmed the ship. He was probably a boy, most trimmers were."

The next three granite stones all signify crew: Steward, G. Simpson; Fireman H. Stewart; Fireman C. Mullen. Then the fifth one: "Unknown Negro, s.s. *Tuscania*, Known unto God." Crew or soldier? Probably crew. There were black mem-

bers of the crew; I remember a newspaper photo of two standing with a group of survivors. All of the soldiers were supposed to have been removed from this cemetery in the twenties either to the United States or to Brookwood Cemetery in England. But there is definitely one soldier still here. On the sixth stone, a marble one, we read: "Private Roy Muncaster, D. Coy., 6th Batt., 20th Engineers, U.S. Army." The forest ranger from Washington, a member of Percy's company. The other five graves hold the remains of five warriors from World War II: two sailors, a sergeant in the Pioneer Corps, two RAF pilots.

From my pocket I take out the photograph made by Archibald Cameron of the graveside services held here on 13 February 1918. He took it from a point within this little plot—unwalled then—looking toward the grassy slopes. In the foreground are the mounded graves. The minister, the piper, and the honor guard stand facing the Union Jack and the homemade Stars and Stripes. Beyond them is the wagon on which the coffins were brought here. Holding the photo in my hand, looking at the landmarks in the distance, I move around until I am standing in the exact spot where Cameron snapped his picture. The moment is silent now as it was then. Only the wind whispers, rising and falling, blending with the soughing of tiny waves on the beach below. In the white curve of a dune, nestled down between hummocks of grass, are two lovers. I turn and look south to the scene depicted in the copy of the A. Shanks painting which hung in my room. I see, as he saw then, the circuit of Kilnaughton Bay and in its arc, up from the shore, the old cemetery. I see the white

Kilnaughton Bay and the American cemetery where Percy was first buried.
(Author's collection.)

lighthouse on the point, then the open sea out of which, that stormy February night sixty-two years ago, came the lifeboats. Little has changed—the lighthouse has a fresh coat of paint; the population of the cemetery has grown. That is all.

We walk over to the cemetery and wander around in the long grass between the gravestones. Many of them have stood or lain here for centuries, but now few over 150 years old can be read. Wind and rain have blurred the old inscriptions. On one tall stone Joan reads the tragic history of a family as cursed as any in Sophocles: a son killed in France in December 1915; a month later the father and another son drowned at the lighthouse; a third son dead shortly after birth; a fourth killed in France in 1916; several years later a memorial to the last child, a daughter; finally, the mother's name. Near the seaward wall of the cemetery are the ruins of a small twelfth-century chapel. Wild flowers and ferns grow in the crevices of the stone walls. On the grassy floor, now open to the sky, among the buttercups and daisies, is a massive

Roy Muncaster's grave in the little cemetery at Kilnaughton Bay. (Author's collection.)

Everett's "Buddy"—

stone slab. On it is carved the effigy of a knight. He wears a long, quilted tunic, a cuirass of chain mail covers his breast and a pointed helmet protects his head. His left hand rests on his long sword. Here lies a Crusader.

Monday. On the Oa by a farmer's gate we leave our hired car. A sign directs us to the "American Memorial." We go over a stile, down a slope, over two more stiles, up across a meadow, over another stile, through a field of heather, through a gate, and there, half a mile away at the end of a narrow path worn into the peat, stands the monument. Someone seems to be moving by the plinth. As we get closer we see it is a sheep. The wind is blowing strongly now out of the south, the same wind that blew the *Tuscania*'s lifeboats here. The monument is a cylindrical stone tower ten feet wide and sixty-five feet high, like a lighthouse. On the north side, where the door would be were this a real lighthouse, is a cast iron plaque, six feet high and five feet wide. Perched above it, within a wreath in front of a cross, the American eagle hovers over the inscription, quoted in full on this page.

Amazingly, the plaque is almost untouched by graffiti. (One scratched, evocative date stands out: 1939. The beginning of another war.) Set in the turf on the south side of the monument is a bronze wreath presented by President Wilson in "memory of his fellow citizens who gave their lives for their country in nearby waters." Thirty feet farther the land drops sheer to the sea four hundred feet below. They say that when it is clear you can see Rathlin Island eighteen miles to the south. Not today. Here Robert Morrison and Duncan Campbell helped the survivors up the cliffs. Three miles west, fifty fathoms down, lies the *Tuscania*. During the three hours that she had remained afloat after being torpedoed she, like the lifeboats, had been carried northward by wind and tide. She drifted almost thirteen miles before she sank.

We walk east along the bluff a quarter of a mile and look down on a small bay, Port nan Gallan.

Burial of American soldiers at Kilnaughton Bay, 13 February 1918. Percy was buried here. The balding man to the left of the minister (reading the service) is probably Hugh Morrison who gave the timber from his estates for the coffins. The American flag is the one made by the five residents of Islay. (Photo-postcard by Archibald Cameron, author's collection.)

Here some soldiers scrambled ashore and here some who did not make it were buried. Offshore, the sea writhes ominously for a thousand yards over the hidden reefs on which lifeboats foundered. Across the bay from the headland where we stand is a higher one, Dun Athad. Beyond it is the great bulk of Beinn Mhor, the highest cliff on Islay. Like visitors to a crumbling Greek amphitheater we gaze in silence, pondering the tragedy played out on this vast stage.

"Here's where Percy ceased being a kid and became a Hero," I say to Joan.

"What a waste it was. Do you think he 'gave' his life for his country?"

"'*Dulce et decorum est pro patria mori*'? No. But he did what he had to do."

The Crusader's grave in the old cemetery at Kilnaughton Bay. (Author's collection.)

That evening we knock on the door of 85 Frederick Crescent. This is the house where Jetty Shanks sheltered Ed Brownell and six other survivors. The door is opened by her "little nephew called Islay," and his wife, Annette. "I always thought of myself as a big boy," laughs Islay as we settle down in their second-floor living room. Islay, now seventy-three, is a retired school teacher from Glasgow. Thin, wiry, a bit creaky in the joints, he is articulate and witty. Annette is younger, very fit, alert, a no-nonsense sort of person with a twinkle in her eye. Islay puts me on his

The American Memorial on the Mull of Oa. (Author's collection)

Everett and I stood here and read the commerating lines on Monument.

59

The American Memorial on the Mull of Oa, looking east to Port nan Gallan. The lifeboats were smashed against these cliffs. (Author's collection)

right, nearest his hearing aid. "Jetty Shanks was my aunt, my father's sister. She taught all her life in Port Ellen School. Her sister, Bella, kept house. They were a lively pair. As a boy I used to come from Glasgow and spend summers here. Bella had Gaelic. So did my father. But Jetty didn't."

Islay "has" Gaelic, too. Joan tells him we went out to the Mull of Oa and asks him what Oa means.

"The quickest answer is nobody really knows," he says, "but after that, one guess is it's a Gaelic corruption of 'Otha,' a Norse word meaning buri-

SACRED
TO THE
IMMORTAL MEMORY
OF THOSE
AMERICAN SOLDIERS AND SAILORS
WHO GAVE THEIR LIVES
FOR
THEIR COUNTRY
IN THE
WRECKS OF THE TRANSPORTS
"TUSCANIA" AND "OTRANTO"
FEBRUARY 5TH 1918 — OCTOBER 6TH 1918
THIS MONUMENT WAS ERECTED BY
THE AMERICAN NATIONAL RED CROSS
NEAR THE SPOT WHERE SO MANY OF
THE VICTIMS OF THE DISASTERS
SLEEP
IN
EVERLASTING PEACE

"On Fame's Eternal camping ground
Their silent tents are spread
While Glory keeps with solemn round
The bivouac of the dead."

The bronze tablet on the American Memorial. (Author's collection)

Port nan Gallan. (Author's collection.)

al mound. In 1918 Gaelic was pretty commonly spoken on Islay. One boat was smashed on the rocks not far from where the monument is now. Some managed to scramble up the cliffs in the dark and find a farmhouse. They were a bit disconcerted to hear a 'foreign' language being spoken! But they were taken in and sheltered and the farmer had himself lowered down the face of the cliff on a rope and rescued several of the injured. He got a civilian medal for valor."

Islay unrolls and spreads out a large map. "I used to do a lot of exploring archaeological sites."

The American eagle and wreath above the plaque on the American Memorial. (Author's collection)

Port Ellen, Islay, by moonlight. (Author's collection.)

He chuckles, "It solved a lot of Christmas present problems to get me another sheet of six inch map." I tell him we looked down at Port nan Gallan and he puts his forefinger on the map. "*Gallan* by the dictionary means a branch, or, by metaphor, a tall young man, a hero. So it is either a bay where the driftwood was tree branches, or it was remembered for an occasion when there was a collection of young men there."

"And so it is still.... Now what about 'A. Shanks' who painted the picture of Kilnaughton Bay? Was he your father?"

"Yes. You know that my aunts had some of the survivors in this very room. One of them, seeing

Painting by A. Shanks of Port nan Gallan Bay where thirty-six of the *Tuscania* dead were
temporarily interred. See the photos on pages 50 and 67. (Author's collection.)

some of my father's paintings on the walls here
asked if he could get a picture of the bay. There
were no suitable post cards. So my aunt wrote to
my father in London. He was a private in the Royal Engineers, Postal Section. He went out and
bought a box of paints and sat on the edge of the
bed in his billet and painted a picture of the light-

house and Kilnaughton Bay and sent it off to Jetty.
She gave it to the young lad who had been em-
ployed by the East Bay Water Company in Oak-
field, California."

"Ed Brownell, from Oakland."

"And they printed it in the company magazine,
Bubbles, with a marvelous caption, 'Painted by a

British army officer who was at the scene at the time of the disaster and has since given his life for the cause of democracy on the western front'! Actually, he lived a full and happy life and died at the age of seventy-eight."

I'm aware of a soft but sharp whistle. Islay looks over at his wife. "Yes?"

"I was asking if they'd like to have a drink." She smiles at me. "He can hear that whistle when he can't always hear a voice." I accept a glass of Islay malt and ask Islay if he can remember anything about those events of sixty-two years ago.

"Well, I was in Glasgow when the ship was sunk and I didn't come back to the island until the summer after the war, when I was twelve. I remember my parents and others talking about it. One of the lifeboats was hauled up to the green above the beach. She was there that summer, maybe 1920 as well. We used to play at boats on her. But I do recollect a Dutch coaster from Groningen loading long, white packing cases at the pier. That was 1922, I think. They were taking the bodies back to the States. I remember thinking I should have a feeling of horror, but no, I was just interested."

"What about Roy Muncaster? Do you know why he was left here?"

"There was a rumor that some of the parents came over and when they saw the actual burial place they gave orders to leave their sons there. It's a beautiful site."

"Yes. But he's the only American soldier still buried at Kilnaughton."

"Did you see the grave of the Unknown Negro?"

I say I had, and explain why I think he was probably a member of the crew.

Islay hands me a sheet of paper from a file on the table. "Here's something that was written by a local woman, Roslyn Mitchell, about 1930. It's a sort of poem." (See page 68.)

I hand him back the poem. "I never thought of my Uncle Percy as a Crusader."

"Roslyn Mitchell did. I think everyone in that generation did."

I think about that. I remember now Wilson's war to "make the world safe for democracy" and Humbleton's "America must save the world." I remember Pastor Stewart's commencement speech to Percy's class, "a great service stretches out before you," and A. W.'s accolade to the *Tuscania* dead, "Above their tomb new western chivalry / Rides to fulfill their prayer." I remember the painting of Sir Galahad that Percy's schoolmates chose for his memorial. And I remember the gold star that hung on the wall of Grannie's bedroom the day she set out to cross the continent and the ocean to find the grave of her warrior son.

Port nan Gallan Bay. The flag made by the five Islayians (see photo p. 49) stands by the thirty-six graves. Three or four wrecked lifeboats are on the beach. (See painting, p. 65 and photo p. 32.) (National Archives)

The Two Crusaders

On February 5, 1918, the liner
"Tuscania," bearing soldiers of the
United States to Europe, was sunk by a
German submarine near the rugged
rocks of the Oa.

In time the bodies of the men were
washed ashore in the bay and were laid
to rest in this little graveyard by the
sea, specially prepared for them,
and there they lay in peace;
British sailors, American soldiers,
and the Negro Unidentified.

In time the citizens of the United States
sent over a Commission to bring back to
America
the bodies of their young citizens.
Reverently the young soldiers were
removed. The Negro unidentified was left.

At the point of the Oa the women of the
United States reared a great tower from
which the American Eagle spreads his
mighty wings in honour of the young
white crusaders, but the Unknown
Warrior whose ancestors British slavedealers
shipped to America still lies
beside the sea—but not alone.

In the ancient Churchyard fifty yards away
there lies another Unknown Warrior. His
grave is marked by a large slab of stone on
which is carved the figure of a Crusader
of the olden time, in full armour.
None can tell who he was save that he was
an ancient chief who went forth from the
Isle to the Holy Land and came back to
the little green place beside the Golden
Sands. Centuries of time span those
fifty yards between the Unknown Crusader
and the Negro Unidentified.

If I were a citizen of the United States
I would go back and tell the people
of the companionship of those two Crusaders
and I should ask my friends
to join me in setting up over the grave
of the Negro Unidentified a statue
in black marble of a Negro looking
from the Isle of the Hebrides
over the sea that leads to Africa and America.
It would then be that just as all
who see the Crusader in the old Kirkyard
link up the centuries as they look upon his figure,
so would all who should see the Negro
link up three races and three continents
in the figure of the Unknown African Negro
who came from America
for the salvation of Europe.

The grave of the "unknown Negro" at Kilnaughton Bay. (Author's collection.)

PILGRIMAGE

Gold Star Mothers arriving at one of the American cemeteries in France. They carry the flowers they will place on their sons' graves. (National Archives.)

GOLD STAR LEGISLATION

At the time my father embarked for France with the American Expeditionary Forces (AEF) in November 1917, my mother and grandmother hung a blue star in the window of their home in Bend. Then, when my uncle Percy, their eighteen year-old brother and son, enlisted in the 20th Engineers and sailed for France on the liner *Tuscania* in February 1918, a second blue star joined the first. On their breasts, too, they pinned the blue star, proud symbol that their men were serving in the armed forces of their country.

In December 1917 American troops had been at the front for two months. There had been casualties and some bereaved families had exchanged the blue star for a black arm band or dress. The prospect that more Americans would be wearing black as the casualties increased was beginning to cause concern. A month earlier the chairman of the Women's Committee of the Illinois State Council of Defense had proposed that the country adopt some symbol other than the traditional black. "Soldiers do not like it," she said, "and

Germany forbids it. The glory of the dead should be emphasized rather than the sadness." She suggested that a gold star would be more appropriate. The *New York Times* concurred. Death in the country's good cause, wrote the editor, is an "honor rather than a misfortune. There is no better death than this and none so good, and manifestation of its glory rather than of private grief becomes the patriotic citizen." The public agreed. When Percy died in the torpedoing of the *Tuscania* in February 1918, his friends presented his sisters and mother with the memorial gold star that hung on Grannie's bedroom wall for so many years. President Woodrow Wilson made the symbol official in May.

Any American who had lost a relative in the war was entitled to wear or display a gold star in place of the blue one. There could have been, then, Gold Star brothers and sisters, Gold Star aunts and uncles, Gold Star grandparents and Gold Star fathers. But after May 1918, the label was rarely applied to any but mothers.

This was largely because of an idea born in the Paris office of the AEF newspaper, *Stars and Stripes*. That spring the editors originated and promoted a campaign to get every soldier in France to write to his mother on Mother's Day, 12 May. Mother's Day was then in its infancy. It had been conceived by Anna M. Jarvis in Philadelphia in 1913 and declared a national holiday by President Wilson the following year, but until 1918 the day and the mothers had received little national attention. The *Stars and Stripes* plan was quickly picked up by the army and the press. "I wish," declared Commander-in-Chief of the AEF, General John J. Pershing, "every officer and soldier in the American Expeditionary Forces would write a letter home on Mother's Day." In order to help the half-million Americans in France to carry out the General's wish, Young Men's Christian Association (YMCA) personnel distributed stationery to the troops and handed out special "Mother's Booklets" containing, for the pencil chewers, a "typical letter written by any soldier to any mother" and, to set the mood, two poems: Kipling's "Mother O'Mine" and Henry Van Dyke's "A Prayer for a Mother's Birthday." The title of Kipling's poem is taken from the refrain which appears in the second and fourth verses of every stanza:

If I were drowned in the deepest sea
    Mother O' Mine, Mother O' Mine,
I know whose tears would come down to me
    Mother O' Mine, Mother O' Mine!

In Van Dyke's poem the speaker offers a prayer on his mother's birthday:

I cannot pay my debt
For all the love that she has given;
But thou, love's Lord,
    wilt not forget
Her due reward—bless her in earth
    and heaven.

On the home front President Wilson asked his fellow citizens to be conscious of "the patriotic sacrifices which are being so freely and generously made by the mothers of our land in unselfishly offering their sons to bear arms, and, if need be, to die in defense of liberty and justice," and especially to "remember those mothers in our prayers, praying God for his divine blessing upon them and upon their sons whose whole-hearted service is now given to the country which we love." Secretary of the Navy Josephus Daniels reminded Americans "that the morale of a nation's soldiers and the ideals for which they fight are born in the spiritual heroism of a nation's mothers." From France, where he was inspecting the troops, Secretary of War Newton Baker cabled to the mothers: "to you they send a message filled with determination and with hope . . . to make this war the last war that America will ever have to fight."

Since this Mother's Day happened to fall on the same Sunday that France traditionally honored Joan of Arc, the American mothers were included in the prayers that the French offered up to their warrior saint. Mme. Joffre, wife of Marshal Joffre, commander-in-chief of the Allied armies, wrote to Anna Jarvis, "At this moment an everlasting union is sealed between France and the

United States. Together our sons are shedding their blood, and we mothers, accepting their sacrifice, offer the life of our hearts in the same feeling of absolute confidence in victory." Mme. Poincaré, the French president's wife, in her letter to the founder of Mother's Day, recalled that before the United States entered the war, "American mothers, with tender care, sent us their children's toys to serve for our own ... now they see their sons cross the ocean" alongside the sons of French mothers.

The national and international attention given to the mothers of America that May not only resulted in the New York postal authorities being buried under a million and a half soldiers' letters, but also firmly fixed in the public consciousness that it was the mothers who had sent ("offered") the troops ("our boys") to fight the Germans. No one has said it better than the Gold Star Mothers themselves: "We all know that the World War had come to be known as a Boys' War, and especially is this true of our own American Expeditionary Forces. The great bulk of our forces were composed of the youth of the country.... The nearest and dearest thing on earth to them was mother." Here is the rationale for the legislation that would result in the mothers' pilgrimages to the graves of their sons in Europe.

When the war ended in November there were many active local and state women's war organizations and a few that claimed national status, such as the National War Mothers, and the National Association of Mothers of Defenders of Democracy. Out of these grew several Gold Star Mothers groups, the first of which seems to have been the Gold Star Mothers of Rochester, New York, Corps No. 1, organized in 1918 by Ida M. Evans. This was followed by, among others, the Order of the Gold Star in Howard, Kansas, the National Association of Gold Star Mothers in Staunton, Virginia (President Wilson's birthplace), and the Gold Star Mothers Association of America in Richmond Hill, New York. In 1928 a group of mothers in Washington, D.C. took out articles of incorporation and formed what was to become, and still is, the recognized national organization, American Gold Star Mothers, Inc.

Eventually most of the other groups across the country either disbanded or merged with the Washington mothers. But a recruitment letter ("In Unity There Is Strength. Come Out And Join Us"), sent out by American Gold Star Mothers, suggests that there had been some in-fighting along the way to unity: "We will be looking for you to become a member. In joining be careful that you place your membership in the right organization as there are various small groups who have accomplished nothing who are trying to form organizations and really conflict at times with our organization."

This same letter gave to Mathilda Burling, by then president of American Gold Star Mothers, the credit for getting Congress to pass the Gold Star Mothers Pilgrimage Act of 1929. And with good reason. However, the first of many efforts to persuade the government to pay for the transportation to Europe of the Gold Star Mothers was made in 1919 by Representative Fiorello H. La Guardia of New York. The flamboyant La Guardia, who fifteen years later was to become New York City's mayor, sponsored a bill that would have paid ocean transportation for both parents to the grave of their son. It never reached the floor for a vote but the seed of the plan had been planted. Although there was no legislative action the following year, the press printed stories sympathetic to the mothers and their wishes to travel to their sons' graves: at Mother's Day exercises in Central Park, forty-eight Gold Star Mothers were guests of honor; in Wilmington, Delaware, a Gold Star Mother christened a cargo ship the *Gold Star*; from Ways Station, Georgia, Mamie Taylor wrote to the editor of the *New York Times* that she was anxious to go to France to the grave of her son but dreaded going alone; and from Britain, a former Tommy's mother wrote that she would gladly visit and photograph for any American mother the grave of "her dear lad" buried across the sea.

In 1921 the Gold Star Mothers of Philadelphia announced that they would ask Congress to give Gold Star Mothers traveling expenses to go to the graves of their sons in France, and late that autumn a group of mothers met with President Harding to discuss the plan. Out of this conference came a bill that Representative Hamilton Fish of New York submitted to Congress on 12 December. Fish's bill asked for "ocean transportation for parents and wives of certain deceased persons who lost their lives during the World War and are buried overseas." Congress referred it to its Committee on Military Affairs. Five days later Fish introduced the bill again, and on 21 December John Jacob Rogers of Massachusetts put it to

the House a third time. The congressmen handed the bill down to the committee and adjourned for the holidays.

The bill died in committee, but the sentiment behind it was given another public boost in 1923 when the American Battle Monuments Commission was created as an independent agency of the United States government, with General Pershing chairman. Serving with the other five male members from the House, the Senate, the National Guard, the American Legion, and the Veterans of Foreign Wars, was one woman, a Gold Star Mother. In March 1924, the Commission sailed for Europe to make plans for the construction of memorial chapels at military cemeteries already established by the War Department. Just a month earlier, the Gold Star Mothers had again picked up the torch and persuaded Representative Sam Dickstein of New York to introduce a bill similar to Fish's. This time the bill attracted the attention of the secretary of war. Unfavorable attention. Secretary John W. Weeks told Congress that the War Department did not have the money and could not furnish the ships. Even if it could, he said, army transports would not be economical: to send the mothers to Europe on them would cost $400 each, whereas they could go for only $270 on civilian vessels. In any case, he insisted, the military personnel could not be spared. The congressmen listened to Weeks and then sent the bill to another slow and languishing death in the Military Affairs Committee.

This time there was a mother at the bill's bedside: Mother Burling was in Washington with a delegation of twenty Gold Star Mothers. And by

29 May they had succeeded in persuading Representative John McKenzie of Illinois to sponsor H.R. 9538 to provide for the transportation to Europe of mothers only. The Sixty-eighth Congress, following the now familiar pattern, gave the bill to the committee, expecting to be rid of it, only to see it come bouncing back the next day with the committee's blessing. Mathilda Burling and her twenty supporters had been busy. Their hopes must have faded, though, when the summer passed and the bill was not put on the House calendar. But they did not quit. In November they bravely announced that the first group of mothers would be sailing the following May. That winter, having learned the ways of the natives, they energetically lobbied, so that by January 1925, they had found another champion of their cause in Henry L. Jost, representative from Missouri. During a debate in the House on an appropriations measure, Jost asked for and was granted nine minutes to speak for the mothers. His remarks that day easily stand as one of the classic panegyrics on the institution of American motherhood.

Jost began by explaining that he had been asked to say a "word" on behalf of McKenzie's bill by a "large number of splendid women . . . quite a few wearing the honorable insignia of the gold star." He reminded his colleagues that as a member of the House he had sat for days listening to the arguments for the claims made by sugar brokers and war contractors for the losses they sustained under war contracts.

But, gentlemen, are dollars all there are in the world? Was property only involved in the World War? Did human flesh and suffering count for nothing? Are the tears and mental anguish of the mothers of this land whose heartstrings were cut by German bullets of no consequence? Does the jingle of gold and silver interest this Congress more than the heavy heart of a mother who, after having gone down into the valley and risked her life, finds the fruit of her suffering cut down in the morning of his existence, and in a grave which for lack of means she has never seen? Is human feeling numb in the House? Have we so trained our minds to think in terms of money that humanitarian problems cease to have any meaning to us? Who was it that suffered sleepless nights during the late war and was up at the break of dawn and out in the yard waiting the coming of the morning paper to read the casualty lists? It was not the sugar broker, it was not the horse and mule buyer, it was not the speculator in war provisions. Nay, it was none of these. It was the frail, nervous little mother who was out there reaching atremble for that paper, hesitant to read it when she picked it up for fear that the name of her boy might be in the list. And yet we are ready to hear and to push and allow the claims on our calendar, the while remaining indifferent to the plaintive request of these mothers.

At this time Jost was interrupted by Fiorello La Guardia: "Will the gentleman yield?"
Jost: "My time is about up."
La Guardia: "I introduced a bill in the Sixty-

sixth Congress upon that subject and could not even get a hearing upon it."

Jost:

Mr. Chairman, it has somehow slipped our minds that it was the mothers of this land who furnished the millions of soldiers for the American battle line [applause], and that it was their contribution, their sacrifice, and their sorrow that made the Stars and Stripes triumphant. And what do we ask? Not money, for theirs was a gift to the Nation. They do not seek indemnity, because theirs was a loss which cannot be measured in dollars. . . . They seek to have accorded to each sorrowing mother whose boy still sleeps in Flanders Field the poor and sad privilege to go there and embrace the earth that encloses his silent and wasting form and cry over it a little while. . . . Oh, what an overwhelming duty we owe to her who laid and lost upon the altar of this Republic the immediate jewel of her life. She it was who paid the price for victory. The sympathy and the gratitude should be hers without the asking. She has won a higher rank than that of a suppliant.

Think of this one moment more, I pray you. Of all the splendid relationships you have known in life is there any one of them that can transcend that which springs from the travail of her who first put her arms about you? Is there any other word in the English language that gathers and expresses more of life than the word "mother"? Is there anything so pure and so sweet as a mother's kiss? Is there any interest so unselfish and so genuinely true as that of a mother? Surely he who has been warmed as a boy and into manhood by a mother's love is blessed of God. . . . Please gentlemen, be considerate of and just to the mothers of our soldier dead. May I not ask you again to interest yourselves in [the bill] to which I have referred, and may I not alone declare my conviction that to adjourn without passing [it] will eternally disgrace this Congress.

Having used up his nine minutes Jost sat down and the House resumed its debate on appropriations. No more was said about the bill that year. But just as Mrs. Burling had predicted, some Gold Star Mothers did sail for Europe in May, although not as guests of the government. The women who boarded the *George Washington* on the thirteenth paid the United States Lines $225 each for transportation to France and a visit to the cemeteries.

As 1925 ran out, two final attempts were made to get Congress to act. Representative Dickstein again submitted his bill on 7 December, and Hamilton Fish his fifteen days later, but the legislators left the bills on the table and went home for Christmas, just as in 1921 and 1924. Although these unsuccessful attempts appeared to have sapped the mothers' strength, since no bills were submitted to Congress in 1926, in actuality they were hard at work preparing for their next big offensive, the ninth and final one. This one, like so many that had failed before, was made in the winter, in December 1927, when Representative Thomas S. Butler of Pennsylvania submitted H.R.

5494. Under his plan the government would pay the transportation of the mother from her home to the cemetery in Europe or, if she were dead, of another member of the deceased soldier's family. As usual the bill was sent down to the Committee on Military Affairs and when in February 1928, the committee met to consider it, Mathilda Burling was prepared. Having secured an invitation to appear as a witness, she arose and addressed the committee members:

Have you gentlemen stopped to think and consider what America would have done if it had not been for these mothers? Not alone the gold-star mothers, but all the mothers who gave their sons to serve their country. It was the mothers who suffered to bring these boys into the world, who cared for them in sickness and health, and it was our flesh and blood that enriched the foreign soil.

Can you picture the anxiety of these mothers watching at the door for the postman every day for that little letter that was to come from her boy, and the agony and suspense when those letters stopped, and then only to be replaced with a telegram from Washington informing her that her boy was wounded or missing or dead?

Many of these boys were just in the bloom of life, just going into manhood. Some of the mothers lost one, some two, and some three and some four.

I would like to take my case for example. On February 13 it will be the tenth anniversary of the death of my boy. He was my only child. To me he was only a child, only seventeen years old when he went across. He was killed when to me life was sweetest, only to have been turned to sorrow at the receipt of the dreadful telegram announcing his death. There were many nurses who were with the boys when they died. They have informed mothers that the boys' lips were sealed with the words "Mother, my Mother." Oh, what a death, to be calling for his mother!

Can a government ever repay us for our loss? The cost of this pilgrimage would be very little for the government to do for us. It would only be fitting to send us across this year, this being the tenth anniversary of our great sacrifice, and I am sure it would not be asking too much. May we not include the mothers of the unknown dead on this trip? There are so few. The government has done such good work in identifying the bodies. I believe there are only about 300 left. What a comfort it would be to let these mothers kneel at one of the graves marked with a marble cross with the words, 'Here lies an honored American soldier known but to God,' and be comforted thinking it might be her boy!

Gentlemen, think of those dear, sweet mothers now on in years. This might be granting their last wish. Many have died with a broken heart. Can those who remain not be given this comfort of going over? Does it not seem a shame that the mothers have to beg for that privilege which should have been offered to them?

"Mother Burling's Plea" (as it came to be called) lacked the rhetorical flourish of Jost's speech, but perhaps for that reason, and because it was given by a Gold Star Mother, it succeeded where his had failed. In an action unprecedented in the history of the committee, the members voted on and unanimously passed the bill while Mrs. Burling and the other witnesses were still in the room.

The House then passed it on 20 February and sent it on to the Senate—which sent it down to its Committee on Military Affairs. There it sat until 7 May when someone finally asked the chairman, Hiram Bingham of Connecticut, when the bill would be considered. Soon, he replied.

When three more weeks slipped by without any action, W. H. McMaster, the senator from South Dakota, demanded that the bill be taken from the committee and acted upon by the Senate. No, said Bingham: the bill was extremely controversial and had generated much discussion. Fathers, he said, claimed the right to be included; there were mothers who said they could not go unless their children were allowed to accompany them; mothers of permanently disabled soldiers objected to money being spent for this purpose; mothers whose sons were buried in the United States (at Arlington, for example) wanted to be included; the American Legion said that the bill was "unwise"; and there were those who questioned the bill's constitutionality. So Bingham was permitted to take it back to his committee, which labored on it for nine months, until February 1929, when he brought it back to the Senate.

After defeating an amendment that would have included mothers of soldiers buried in the United States, the Senate passed the bill within a week. The day after the Senate acted the House swiftly passed the legislation and on 2 March 1929, President Hoover signed "The bill to enable mothers and widows of the American forces interred in the cemeteries of Europe to make a pilgrimage to these cemeteries." Thus, almost twelve years and four administrations after La Guardia first presented the plan to the House, the Gold Star Mothers saw their wish become an act of Congress.

THE
ACT AND
CONTROVERSY

It is March 1929. Spring in Washington, D.C. Winter still hangs on in central Oregon. Life went on quietly in the brick house on Broadway in Bend, where I lived with my father and mother, and two of my brothers, Frank, thirteen, and John, four. My older brother, George, sixteen, was away at school. I was six.

Of course there was Grannie. I remember her rocking in her chair by a sunny window, crocheting or darning socks, sometimes pausing to offer me one of her tiny licorice cough pastilles, Lilliputian black pillows taken from a thin, tin box. When I saw the paper boy coming up the street and heard the "thunk" as the rolled-up *Bend Bulletin* hit the front door, I would run and bring it to Grannie. It was in one of these March *Bulletin*'s, eleven years after her son died in the sinking of the *Tuscania*, that Grannie must have learned about the Gold Star Mother legislation that would make it possible for her to visit his grave.

Under the provisions of the Act a "mother" was defined not only as she who gave birth to the soldier buried overseas but also as "stepmother, mother through adoption, or any woman who stood in loco parentis to the deceased member of the military or naval forces for the year prior to the commencement of his service in such forces." Widows who had not remarried also were eligible. The son or husband must have died between 15 April 1917 (nine days after war was declared) and 1 July 1921 (the day before the peace treaty with Germany was officially signed). He must be buried in Europe. However, before the pilgrimages began, an amendment was attached to the Act which also qualified mothers and widows of soldiers and sailors missing in action. Women who had already been able to visit their sons' or husbands' graves (such as those who had taken the United States Lines trip in 1925) were ineligible. The pilgrimages were to be made between 1 May 1930 and 31 October 1933, on American ships. American citizens were to be issued special passports. Resident aliens would be issued travel documents that would allow them to reenter the country regardless of immigration restrictions. All expenses would be paid: railroad fare to New York City, hotel accommodations there, cabin class passage to Europe, hotel and transportation charges during the two weeks abroad, and all meals. In addition, each woman was to be given a generous per diem allowance of $10. (In 1930, ordinary government officials received $4.00, higher ones $6.00.)

The secretary of war was directed to determine, and to report to Congress by 15 December, the total number of mothers and widows entitled to make the pilgrimage, how many of these desired to go, and how many wanted to go in 1930. He was also asked to make an estimate of the cost of the pilgrimages. Acting Secretary of War Patrick J. Hurley had all of this information by 6 December. In his letter of transmittal to the speaker of the House, he reported that there were 11,440 eligible mothers and widows, 6,730 who desired to make the pilgrimage, and 5,323 who wanted to go in 1930. The probable cost, based upon his estimate of $840 for each woman, would be $5,653,200. Hurley also submitted a booklet giving the names of all eligible mothers and widows, together with their wishes as to whether and when they wanted to go and the names and burial locations of their sons and husbands.

Both the House and the Senate voted the first week of February 1930 to appropriate the money. At a White House ceremony on 8 February, the wife of President Herbert Hoover drew lots from a silver bowl to determine the mothers' order of departure, by states. Nebraska was first, with 59 planning to go the first year, Colorado with 64 was last. New York led the list in numbers with 742, followed by Pennsylvania with 597, California, 369, Massachusetts, 318, and Ohio, 282. Puerto Rico and Hawaii had a single mother each. Hurley's report did not indicate how many of the 11,440 eligible women were mothers and how many widows, but mothers outnumbered widows by a large majority because, in 1918, most of the "boys" were unmarried and by 1929 most of the widows had remarried.

How did Hurley arrive at the figure of 11,440 women eligible to make the pilgrimage? The explanation goes back twelve years to 1918 when, two months before the Armistice, the War Department had announced that the bodies of all servicemen buried in Europe would be returned to the United States, just as they had been in 1898 when soldiers killed in the war with Cuba had been brought home for burial. But shortly after the Armistice the War Department had backed off from this policy, largely because of the objections of Colonel Teddy Roosevelt, hero of San Juan Hill, former president of the United States. Roosevelt's youngest son, Quentin, an aviator, had been shot down over German lines in July and buried where he fell, near Chambray. Roosevelt wrote to General P.C. March, Army chief of staff, asking that Quentin's body be left in French soil: "Let the young oak lie where it fell." March honored Roosevelt's request and asked General Pershing to do the same for any other next of kin who might share Roosevelt's feelings.

Roosevelt's letter and March's response generated discussion and controversy that continued throughout 1919. In January 1920, the *New York Times* headline read:

Grannie Stevens with her daughter Mabel, and three of her grandchildren. The author is holding the cat. The date is 1930, the year she made her pilgrimage. (Author's collection.)

Objections to Bringing Home Soldier Dead. In Spite of Fourteen Bills in Congress in Favor of It Some Sentiment Is Against the Practicality of the Plan on a Large Scale.

This headline pretty accurately summed up the country's attitude, and the negative sentiment had been intensified by an article in *The Casket* that had been given wide publicity in newspapers across the nation and even on the floor of Congress. *The Casket*, which claimed to be a periodical for "the higher education of funeral directors, embalmers, and sanitarians," had offered some timely advice to its subscribers: "This is a plain business talk," wrote "S.G.Q.", a "matter of dollars and sense, plus sentiment." S.G.Q. reminded his readers that more than fifty thousand Americans were buried in "alien soil," and that Representative T.H. Caraway of Arkansas was sponsoring a bill to return these dead. "Congress will vote on the bill favorably if enough pressure of public opinion is brought to bear. Extra business, gentlemen, sympathetic, remunerative, extra business. The Congress pauses in its vote to hear the expression of the public's wishes. What are you going to do about it?" The *Stars and Stripes* called the article "atrocious" and congressional opponents of the bill cited it with rhetorical flights of outrage and revulsion, finally prompting John Martin, president of the National Funeral Directors Association, to protest that, "There has not been and is not now any organized effort to urge the bringing back of these bodies."

The *New York Times*, which at the beginning had taken a neutral stand, had by January come down solidly on the side of those who were opposed to returning the bodies: "There is no doubt that the weight of intelligent public opinion opposes the removal. The sentimental campaign for the return of the bodies, however, has had the effect of solidifying a majority of Congress and even the War Department behind the plan." That same month the War Department released the results of a survey. It had sent out 74,720 cards, one to every person whom the servicemen now buried in Europe had listed as next of kin. Of the 63,708 responses received, 43,900, nearly seventy percent, indicated that they did want the bodies returned. Clearly, sentiment was with the War Department. The bill that Congress finally passed in the spring of 1920 authorized the expenditure of public funds to pay for the exhumation and return to this country of the bodies of all soldiers, sailors, airmen, and marines whose next of kin so desired, and for one relative to go to Hoboken, New Jersey, to meet the body and accompany it to its final resting place. The *New York Times* estimated that the cost would be eight million dollars.

A Graves Registration crew landed on Islay in July. The Laird of Islay pleaded for the bodies to remain on his island, promising to look after them "forever," but the Americans pitched their tents on the green pastures by Kilnaughton Bay and started digging. On Sundays they entertained the astonished islanders with exhibitions of baseball; weekdays, children like Islay Shanks watched with curiosity the white boxes being swung onto the ship tied up at the pier. But Percy's body was not one of them. Not then. Those bodies were to be shipped to Hoboken.

Except from a few remote places such as Islay, most of the servicemen's bodies whose relatives had requested that they remain in Britain had already been removed to Brookwood cemetery south of London. Those who had died in Belgium had been buried in Flanders Field, and the Americans who had fallen and been hastily buried in over eight hundred locations in France had been reinterred in one of the six military cemeteries established there. Planted with trees and shrubs, landscaped with lawns and flowers and gravel walks, these cemeteries were, by 1921, already places of great beauty. In April two best-selling American authors, Owen Wister and Thomas Nelson Page, visited these cemeteries where the bodies were being exhumed. They were appalled by what they saw. Both wrote letters which the *New York Times*, still opposed to the scheme, printed on its front page. The older writer, Page, whose theme was often antebellum chivalry, said of the well-kept cemeteries that "no more impressive tribute to American valor and American love of freedom can be imagined," and he cited with approval the sentiment of General Robert E. Lee who "felt the fittest resting place of a soldier was the field of honor on which he nobly laid down his life." Wister's letter, like his novels (e.g. *The Virginian*), sounded a less romantic note. Pointing to the gruesome fact that many of the dead had been buried not in coffins but in blankets or baskets, he described the exhumation of "things without shape at which mothers would collapse." The once-beautiful cemeteries, he wrote, were beginning to look like "old mouths, half teeth, half gum. Can nothing stop this hideous mockery of the living and the dead?" But the work continued. Finally, on 1 April 1922, the body of the last soldier was returned to the United States and buried at Arlington National Cemetery. A month later in keeping with the War Department's policy to bury all of the 30,792 soldiers whose bodies were to remain in Europe in one of the eight American military cemeteries, Percy's body was moved from Islay to Brookwood, its final resting place.

Gold Star Mothers arriving in Paris. (National Archives.)

THE PILGRIMAGE BEGINS

At the time Acting Secretary of War Patrick Hurley was asked to advise Congress in 1929 how many mothers and widows wanted to make the pilgrimage to Europe, he had directed Quartermaster General J. L. DeWitt to write to the next of kin to each of the thirty thousand men buried in France, Belgium, and England. About forty percent of these letters were returned marked "Address Unknown." Nine years had passed since the War Department had communicated with these persons about the burial of their dead. By 1930 many of the older mothers had died, widows had remarried and moved. So DeWitt gave the twelve thousand undelivered letters to the Veterans Bureau to locate the addresses of any who were receiving compensation, and their letters were then sent out again. In addition to the efforts of the War Department, the American Legion, the Veterans of Foreign Wars, the Gold Star Mothers, other patriotic societies, and the press all publicized the plan, "so it seems reasonable to believe," Hurley could report to the speaker of the House, "the matter has been brought to the attention of all persons who are entitled to the benefits of the Act."

By February 1930, when Mrs. Hoover drew Nebraska's name from the silver bowl, the War Department had just about worked out the logistics of transporting over six thousand mostly elderly women to France, looking after them there for two weeks, and carrying them home again. It was a formidable task. The Quartermaster Corps' (QMC) experience in having moved two hundred times that many soldiers to France only twelve years before had not been forgotten and would be useful for this job. However, there must have been some QMC veterans who grumbled that in terms of difficulty the ratio of one Gold Star Mother to two hundred doughboys was just about right. After all, one could not expect these passengers to take orders barked out by a company sergeant, nor could they be fed the "slum" that had been served the troops on the *Tuscania*. It was thought that the average age of the mothers would be sixty; in actual fact it turned out to be sixty-seven. Anticipating illnesses and deaths among its prospective charges, the army asked life insurance companies to give them some statistics. The estimates were gloomy: for the five thousand women that were planning to go in 1930 the insurance men warned the army to expect eight thousand hospital days and sixty-five deaths.

In April the army dispatched Captain Blanche Rulan, assistant superintendent of the Army Nurse Corps, to Paris to prepare hospital facilities and to assemble a group of American and French nurses. She was followed by fifty army officers whose job it would be to escort the pilgrims in small groups during the two weeks they were in Europe. Prohibition followed these soldiers. Before they sailed they were sternly warned that any man touching a drop of liquor, beer, or wine, "even in a home," would be sent back forthwith. In Paris Captain Rulan and the officers met Colonel Richard T. Ellis at his "Pilgrims Headquarters." To Ellis fell the task of planning all the arrangements in France and England. He made the hotel reservations in Paris and at the towns near the cemeteries, he hired the buses that would carry the women to the cemeteries, he selected the civilian translators and guides from the thousand members of the American Legion Post in Paris, and his wife picked the hostesses who would greet the women at the cemeteries.

On 6 May, 234 Gold Star Mothers and Widows assembled in New York. This first group had come by train from Nebraska, Florida, Delaware, Kentucky, and Ohio, the five states selected first by Mrs. Hoover. Each of the women wore on her breast a medal suspended by a red, white, and blue ribbon from a bar inscribed with her name and state. The medal depicts the American eagle

perched on two flags at the top of a circle around which runs the inscription, "Pilgrimages of Mothers and Widows." In the center is a gold star. In her purse she carried a khaki-colored wallet containing her special travel documents and a card giving the name and rank of her son or husband, the cemetery where he was buried, and the exact location of the grave in that cemetery. Grannie's wallet is here beside me. The travel documents are gone, probably picked up by the immigration authorities on her return, but the card is there, together with that graduation photo of Percy. Pinned to the inside flap is her medal. The ribbon is stained from four weeks of wear fifty years ago.

On 7 May the Gold Star Mothers were taken in seven buses to New York's City Hall. (By now, the press was referring to the women as "Gold Star Mothers" or "Mothers." Widows, when there were any, were rarely, if ever, mentioned.) They were greeted by Acting Mayor McKee and Mathilda Burling, now president of American Gold Star Mothers, Inc. McKee read messages from Mayor Jimmy Walker and senators Wagner and Copeland, and then extended the city's official welcome: "Bereavement's accolade," he said, "has raised you to a dignity beyond that attained by princes and kings, and one that makes us proud to honor you."

Following this ceremony the women were taken across to the Jersey side of the Hudson River to Pier No. 4 in Hoboken where they were given a stirring greeting by Legionnaires from New York and New Jersey, the bands of both the Sixteenth Infantry and the Hoboken Police Department, and the Hudson County Legion Drum Corps. As they walked up the gangplank of the ss *America*, white-frocked members of women's auxiliaries presented them with bouquets of poppies and forget-me-nots and small American flags.

After they had found their cabins, more speeches awaited them on deck. They were reminded that it was from this same pier thirteen years ago to the day that the *Orduna* sailed for France with the first American soldiers. "Go, therefore, not in sorrow but in pride," said General Charles Summerville, Army chief of staff. "You leave on this pilgrimage not only as those who were dearest to the men who gave their all for the perpetuation of our democracy. You go also as those who are most worthy to express the gratitude and the eternal memory of our country." Then Paul Chapman, president of United States Lines, whose ships had been selected to carry all the pilgrims to Europe, presented each of the women with a gold medallion inscribed, "Gold Star Pilgrimage to the Battlefields of the World War." Below this is the United States Lines seal. On the reverse, a passenger liner, bathed in the rays of a star, sails from the Statue of Liberty toward the Eiffel Tower. With each medallion came a certificate signed by Chapman and bearing patriotic messages from General Pershing, President Hoover, and President Doumergue of France. When Captain George Fried, veteran of many wartime Atlantic crossings, finally headed the *America* down the river, the ship was accompanied by four fireboats, sirens screaming and spouting high plumes of water. Overhead Army airplanes buzzed and dipped. At the Narrows, Captain Fried signaled a last farewell with a final long blast of the ship's whistle. The pilgrimages had begun.

Ten days later the *America* dropped anchor in Cherbourg harbor. As the tender carrying the mothers approached the quay, they could see the American and French flags flying above the waving and cheering crowds and hear the Cherbourg band, L'Union Lyrique, strike up with the "Star Spangled Banner." On French soil they were welcomed by M. Jules Le Brettevillois, mayor of Cherbourg; M. Quonian, president of the Chamber of Commerce; General Villon of the Union Nationale des Combatants, and the Sous-Préfet, M. Luchaise. Their short speeches were translated by Colonel Ellis's secretary and then the colonel and his staff of doctors, nurses, officers, and translators took the women to their boat train for the journey to Paris. Later that evening they were met at the Gare des Invalides by a representative of the Commission of Tourism who, considerately, greeted the tired ladies with just a brief address before they were taken to their hotels.

The following afternoon a huge multitude awaited the women when they arrived at the Arc de Triomphe to lay a wreath on the tomb of France's Unknown Soldier; the ceremony was attended by French and American generals and admirals, French war mothers and widows, French army veterans, American expatriates, and a hoard of journalists. A contemporary photograph shows the mothers being escorted to the monument by American officers who were garbed in the de ri-

Bronze medal. The bronze medal that the government gave to every one of the 6,600 Gold Star Mothers at the beginning of their pilgrimages in 1930-33 to their sons' graves in Europe. Worn every day while the Mothers were abroad, pinned to their dresses or coats, the medal was both a badge of honor and an identification tag. This is my grandmother's. (Reproduced actual size.)

guer cavalry uniform of the day: riding breeches, tall leather boots, Sam Browne belts buckled across their jackets. The mothers wear ankle-length dresses. Bonnets and cloches protect their gray heads from the warm Parisian sun, many-buttoned spats shield their ankles, white-gloved hands clutch large pocketbooks.

After the ceremony at the Arc de Triomphe, the American ambassador, Walter E. Edge, and his wife, took the ladies to tea at the Restaurant Laurent. When Ambassador Edge introduced General Pershing, the women rose to their feet to applaud their boys' former commander-in-chief. Pershing, chairman of the American Battle Monuments Commission since its creation, assured the mothers and widows that he was devoting all of his time to the care of the final resting places of their sons and husbands. "They served to honor you. They led the clean lives you wished them to. All honor to the mothers of victory."

The eight American military cemeteries in Europe that were under the charge of Pershing's commission are on 285 acres provided rent-free by the governments of France, Belgium, and Britain. Permanent maintenance is paid for by the United States, as was the construction of a chapel and visitor's building at each cemetery. By the time the first group of Gold Star Mothers visited these cemeteries that May of 1930, the ravages that had horrified Wister and Page had healed and the wooden crosses that used to mark the graves had been replaced by marble ones. In 1926 the War Department had budgeted $548,855 for the purchase of these marble crosses and had asked for bids. Congress protested when Secretary of

"On the occasion of the contemplated pilgrimage of the Gold Star Mothers of America to the places where their heroic sons rest, I take the opportunity of addressing to them, in the name of all France, a message of respectful understanding and of cordial welcome"
President Doumergue

"To the patriotic mothers who gave their sons, to the many other loyal women who lost those dear to them for their country's sake ✶ ✶ ✶ ✶ we owe a deep debt of gratitude"
President Hoover

MEDALLION
No. *1683*

Mrs. Laura Stevens

IN MEMORY OF THE SUPREME SACRIFICE WE HAVE THE HONOR TO PRESENT TO YOU THIS GOLD STAR MEDALLION SYMBOLIZING YOUR PILGRIMAGE TO THE BATTLEFIELDS OF THE WORLD WAR

"We silently bow our heads in sympathy with the mothers and widows whose willing gift to the nation was more precious than life itself"
General Pershing

Paul W. Chapman.

The certificate that accompanied the medallion given to all Gold Star Mothers by Paul Chapman, president of United States Lines. This is Grannie's. (Author's collection.)

War Dwight Davis announced that the contract had been awarded to the Societá Anonomia Honoraux of Querceto, Italy, and demanded that American marble or granite should be used. Davis brushed aside these chauvinistic objections, arguing that the crosses of Carrara marble would be more beautiful, more quickly delivered than American stone, and cheaper. Much cheaper— $14.50 each as compared with the American bid of from $78 to $115 each. (Today, after more than

91

An American Indian Gold Star Mother with her companions and French and American army officers. (National Archives.)

fifty years, these crosses are as milky white as the day they were placed on the graves.)

The mothers and widows whose dead were buried at Suresnes, only five miles from Paris, stayed in the city, as did the few whose aviator sons and husbands had died flying for France before 1917 and were buried at the nearby monument to the Lafayette-Escadrille. But most of the pilgrims, after a few days of rest in Paris, traveled in small groups by bus or train to the towns nearest the five cemeteries where their men lay, escorted by one of Colonel Ellis's officers and accompanied by a Legionnaire guide and one or more nurses.

The names of these five cemeteries outside of Paris, all in an arc sweeping from north to east, are a roll call of the great battles in which American units fought from May to November, 1918: Somme, Aisne-Marne, Oise-Aisne, Meuse-

Gold Star Mothers on their way to the tomb of France's unknown soldier at the Arc de Triomphe. Note one mother on crutches. (American Legion Monthly, November 1933.)

Argonne, St. Mihiel. The women whose destination was the Somme stayed in St. Quentin. They were warmly received by the mayor who told them, "For four years we were crushed under the Prussian heel. When the 27th and 30th American Divisions broke the Hindenburg Line at the St. Quentin canal we saw definite signs of our dawning liberation. We forever shall be grateful." There are 1,837 Americans buried here and the names of 333 missing cut into the chapel walls. At Aisne-Marne, fifty-eight miles from Paris, there are 2,288 graves and a memorial to the largest number of missing recorded at any of the cemeteries, 1,060, all victims of the ferocious two-month battle for nearby Belleau Wood. A few miles east, twenty-seven miles southwest of Rheims, is the Oise-Aisne cemetery where 6,012 lie and the chapel lists the names of 214 missing. Farther east still, 152 miles from Paris, is the largest of the American burial grounds, the Meuse-Argonne. Fourteen thousand two hundred forty six white crosses march up a gentle green slope to the chapel on the ridge where 954 missing are remembered. Most of these dead were casualties of a fifty-seven day battle involving twenty-two American divisions (over a million men) and four French divisions, against forty-seven German divisions, a quarter of Germany's strength on the western front. This slaughter ended only with the signing of the Armistice 150 miles away at Compiègné at 11:00 A.M., on 11 November 1918. The women who found their sons and husbands among the 4,152 crosses or the names of the 284 missing at St. Mihiel had the longest journey, 182 miles from Paris. The soldiers who died here in September had been part of an army of 250,000, the largest force, up to that time, solely under American command. In four days they had succeeded in reducing the St. Mihiel salient, driving the Germans out of positions they had been dug into for four years and giving General Pershing his first decisive victory of the war.

Flanders Field at Waragem in Belgium is the smallest of the First World War's American cemeteries, with only 368 graves and a memorial to forty-three missing. But for many Americans it had become the soldier's archetypal resting place, all because of a poem written by a Canadian medical officer, Captain John McCrae, two years before the United States entered the war. The few mothers and widows who traveled to this cemetery in May did indeed find, as I also found when another war took me there in the spring of 1944, that "In Flanders Field the poppies blow / Between the crosses row on row."

At each of these seven cemeteries on the continent and at the eighth in England, the mothers and widows were greeted by the American superintendent of the cemetery, and by Mrs. Ellis's hostesses, who helped them to find the graves they sought. There were no speeches. Each woman was given a wreath of natural flowers and left with her thoughts. The army had expected many incidents of emotional collapse at the graves, but there were few. For the mothers, death was by now a familiar face; most had lost their parents, many had seen brothers, sisters and husbands die. The officers accompanying each group had the military record of every pilgrim's son or husband. He knew the history of the battle in which the soldier had died. After the women had been in the vicinity of the cemetery for two or three days and had made daily visits to the graves, their thoughts turned from their loss to the battles once fought over these peaceful parks where the crosses now stood. Then their guides took them on tours of the battlefields and nearby villages.

For some of the foreign-born Gold Star Mothers there were poignant and sometimes ironic reunions. At the Somme, a mother from Oklahoma knelt at a grave which held her son Gus. Forty-two years before, she had left her home in France with this same son only a ten-month old boy. Gus grew up in America and when his adopted country went to war, he went too. Now he lay within a few miles of the small village where he had been born. In Paris, a mother from Germantown, Pennsylvania, was met by another son who had fought in the

General John J. Pershing.
(National Archives.)

German army at the Battle of the Argonne. An American mother, seventy-one, whose son was killed in the Argonne met her German sister, sixty-seven, whose son had been killed on the Russian front.

As with so many of these mothers, Grannie, too, had been born in Europe. She had left her home in Stavanger, Norway, as a child of seven or eight, with her father and mother Pedersen, four brothers and three sisters, for a new life in Minnesota. Marriage to Fred Stevens had taken her west, first to British Columbia, then to Oregon. She was seventy in 1930 when she accepted her adopted country's invitation to travel to the grave of her youngest son.

So on 21 June 1930, with 280 other Gold Star pilgrims, my grandmother boarded the *President Roosevelt* at Hoboken, New Jersey. After a six-day trip from Bend, first on the Spokane and Seattle Railroad, then the Great Northern, and finally the Pennsylvania, with stopovers in Portland, Chicago, and New York. In two photographs taken of the mothers mustered on the deck of the ship, I find Grannie looking tiny and frail. But she withstood the rigors of the voyage, disembarked on 29 June at Plymouth, an English port memorialized long ago by another group of Pilgrims, and on 1 July she stood in Brookwood cemetery before the cross marking the grave of her son. On it was a wreath sent by the Percy A. Stevens Post of the American Legion in Bend. She and her group of thirty-six were welcomed by Sir Francis Ware, vice chairman of the British Imperial War Graves Commission. An earlier group of mothers had

been greeted at London's Westminster Hall by Lord de Warr, the under secretary for war. This lord with the eponymous name had told the ladies that they were meeting in the same building where the delegates to the recent Naval Conference had assembled, an event, he said, "which might well be found in the future to have laid the foundation for everlasting peace." (The next year Captain Wilhelm Meyer, commander of the U-boat which had sunk Percy's ship, took a somewhat different tone in a letter he wrote to the *Tuscania* Survivors Association: "We Germans and especially we former front line soldiers, do not further desire to live in servitude, and we will hazard everything to bring about the freedom of our people.")

Grannie was in London for eleven days. One afternoon she and her companions were invited to have tea with Lady Astor on a terrace of the Houses of Parliament. Another day she got lost in London, apparently experimenting to see if she could really ride as far as she liked on the trams for just one penny. A sympathetic Irish conductor directed her back to the shopping district.

With the exception of this slight hitch, Grannie's pilgrimage went smoothly from beginning to end. There was, however, one group of mothers whose pilgrimage began under a cloud.

Three months before the first group of Gold Star Mothers was to sail from Hoboken, the National Association for the Advancement of Colored People (NAACP) discovered that black women were to sail on separate ships and be segregated from white women during their entire pilgrimage. When the act to send all Gold Star Mothers had

Some of the 14,246 American graves at the Meusse-Argonne cemetery, 1933. The chapel is on the ridge. (Author's collection.)

been drawn up, one of the stipulations was that no woman could substitute, even at her own expense, transportation or accommodations different from those provided by the government. The mother from the tiny farm in Kansas, the mother from the estate in Long Island, the mother from the remote lumber town in Oregon, rich and poor, citizen and alien, all were to cross the Atlantic cabin class, ride the same buses, and have equal hotel accommodations. However, the act also stipulated that all pilgrimages "shall be made in accordance with such regulations as the Secretary of War may from time to time prescribe as to the time, route, itineraries, program, arrangements, and other matters

General Pershing talking with Gold Star Mothers at an American cemetery in France.
(National Archives.)

pertaining to such pilgrimages." In other words, the women could not change the rules but the War Department could. And did.

The result was that in May, 58 of the 219 black women who had planned to go in 1930 sent a petition to President Hoover protesting:

the gratuitous insult in the attitude of the War Department of the United States in segregating colored Gold Star Mothers.... In the years which have passed since death took our loved ones our anguish and sorrow have been assuaged by the realization that our

Gold Star Mothers mustered on the deck of the S.S. *President Roosevelt*, June 1930. Note the seasick mother in the hatchway. Grannie is on the upper deck, fourth from right.
(Author's collection.)

loved ones who rest in the soil of France gave their lives to the end that the world might be a better place in which to live for all men, of all races and all colors. Twelve years after the Armistice, the high principles of 1918 seem to have been forgotten.

The women appealed to Hoover to abolish the War Department's "Jim Crow" arrangements. If he did not they would respectfully decline to make the trip. Hoover gave the War Department the responsibility of handling the petition. Acting Secretary of War Davis responded that the racial group-

Gold Star Mothers on board the *President Roosevelt*, June 1930. Grannie is in the shade just behind and to the left of the flag. (Author's collection.)

ing had been decided upon "after the most careful consideration of the interests of the pilgrims themselves. No discrimination whatever," Davis said, "will be made as between the various groups. Each group will receive equal accommodations, care and consideration."

In July, Mayor Walker prepared to meet the first group of 104 black Gold Star Mothers at City Hall on the eleventh, but when the day came only 60 showed up. Under fire from the NAACP and even, in a mild way, from the *New York Times* ("Capital rebuffs Gold Star Negroes"), Secretary of War Hurley squirmed but stuck to his separate but equal ruling. "Representatives of the War Department," he said, "will at all times be as solicitous of the welfare of the colored mothers and widows as they will be for the welfare of those of the white race." Referring to the strain that the forthcoming journey would put upon the women, he said that the War Department wished to relieve this by "not disturbing the normal contact of individual pilgrims. It would seem natural to assume that those mothers and widows would prefer to seek solace in their grief from companions of their own race." However, he conceded, the black women could join a white group if the white women agreed, but the condition he attached to this arrangement revealed the extent to which the War Department was deferring to the racial prejudice of the times. "It must be understood," concluded Hurley, "that any change must be predicated on the ability of the War Department to make satisfactory arrangements with the transportation companies and the hotels." The black women "understood." The night of 11 July they slept not in Manhattan hotels but in the Harlem YWCA. The next day Paul Chapman presented each of them with his company's gold medal and certificate and then they sailed on the *American Merchant*, the only Gold Star Pilgrims on the ship.

Colonel Ellis met the group in Cherbourg and took them to Paris where they received a rousing welcome from the large black community that had settled there since the war, many of them musicians, singers, and dancers. At the French Foreign Office a young black woman from a Montmartre cafe pinned an aster on each woman as she mounted the steps for the ceremony there, while Peyton's orchestra from a fashionable restaurant on the Champs Élysées played the American and French national anthems, switching to jazz when the women boarded their buses for the ride to the Impérator, one of Paris's newest hotels. The next day they were greeted at the Arc de Triomphe by the military governor of Paris and a large crowd of black Parisians. Ambassador and Mrs. Edge then took them to tea. The ladies soon discovered, as the blacks who lived there already knew, that "satisfactory arrangements" were easier to make in Paris than in New York.

In spite of the War Department's policy of segregating the black mothers and widows, their pilgrimage seems to have been a success. I can find no record of any comment they made to the War Department, but they sent this testimonial to Paul Chapman, president of United States Lines: "The exquisite cleanliness of the boat and tidiness of the staterooms gave evidence at once of the thoughtfulness of the management. The beautiful and tastefully decorated dining room and delicious food served by spotless and courteous attendants gave proof that somebody meant us to be happy."

Percy Steven's grave in the American Cemetery at Brookwood, England. (Author's collection.)

THE PILGRIMAGE ENDS

All through the summer the troopships *America, Republic, President Harding, President Roosevelt, President Washington*, and the *American Merchant* steamed back and forth across the Atlantic transporting mothers and widows until, on 2 October, the last of 3,653 women stepped ashore at Hoboken. The pilgrimages began again the following May, but the initial rush to go was over. By October of 1931 only 1,766 had made the trip that year, including 40 more black mothers and widows. Five hundred and sixty-six sailed in 1932, and in 1933, the final year, 669, making a grand total of 6,654 transported at government expense to the graves of their sons and husbands, only 76 fewer than Hurley's 1929 estimate.

The hardy pilgrims had made a shambles of the life insurance companies' predictions. Instead of eight thousand hospital days they had required only five hundred, and instead of sixty-five deaths there had been two, only one of them in Europe.

Right up to the final day of the pilgrimages, the doctors and nurses expressed astonishment at the overall endurance of their charges. There was the Texas Gold Star Mother of seventy-five, for example, who broke her hip at the beginning of her train journey in 1931. For months she was immobilized, flat on her back. But she recovered, and made the trip in 1933 on crutches. Then there was Mrs. Elizabeth Hutchins, ninety-two, from Oakland, California, who hopped a Ford Tri-motor airplane, flew across the continent to join her group in New York, crossed the ocean, rode the buses with her companions through France, and returned home as hale as the day she left. One nurse, speculating about the hardiness of the mothers, offered a Darwinian explanation: "They must be the fit that have survived," she said. "Had they been weak they never would have reached their present age."

The strong flesh of the pilgrims and their indomitable spirit won the Army's praise and respect. "Their conduct has been beyond words to express our admiration," said an escorting officer. "Instead of being mournful or depressing to each other, they behaved with a fine bravery which has communicated the courageous attitude of one to another."

The Army pronounced the pilgrimages a success, but objections were raised even before the first group sailed. Those who argued that the bill was too exclusive found a champion in Senator Allen of Kansas who tried, unsuccessfully, to introduce a bill appropriating three and a half million dollars to send fathers. The stock market had crashed in the fall of 1929, only a few months after Hoover had signed the pilgrimage bill, and when the first Gold Star Mothers sailed on the *America* in May 1930, the Great Depression had begun. As it deepened, the objections of those who protested that there were better ways to spend tax dollars intensified: How can the Gold Star Mothers accept these free trips when the Treasury is so depleted?; The pilgrimage bill was a gesture of politicians to get votes; George Washington was willing to give up his salary to help the nation, why not the Gold Star Mothers?; "Is there no way to stop this squandering of public funds in such a manner? ... Many of us are actually hungry and insufficiently clothed, yet, through taxes, we are compelled to pay for these expensive trips."

Defenders of the pilgrimages replied that the mothers had not put the government to the expense of returning their sons' bodies. The pilgrimages in 1933, they said, would cost every American less than the cost of "a penny box of matches ... is that too much?" But for the mothers who had already made the trips, their justification was not to be measured in dollars. "I had mourned the loss of my only child for years and at times was terribly bitter," one mother said. Then she visited the Meuse-Argonne cemetery and found her son sleeping with his comrades. "I realized that others had suffered as I had and that we must try to comfort each other." As a contemporary observer remarked, "There was something in the community of grief that relieved her. And when she saw the care that was given to the graves, she said, 'My country has kept faith.' She returned home with a new-found peace and happiness."

EPILOGUE

May 22, 1980, a Thursday. I drive down a pine-bordered lane with my companions, my wife, Joan and her sister. We turn right at the Memorial Chapel for Canadian soldiers, and pass the graves of the Canadian Military Cemetery on our left, the British Military Cemetery on our right. Another turn and we are at the stone reception building of the four and a half acre Brookwood American Cemetery, twenty-eight miles southwest of London. Through the archway of the low building, shaded by pines and cedars, we can see the green lawn and the white crosses. The visitor's room is furnished with two sofas, several arm chairs, and an oak table. Over the small fireplace hangs a framed purple heart. A plaque explains that this decoration was originated by George Washington and that it had been awarded to every American soldier and sailor buried here. There are framed photographs of generals Pershing and Marshall, American Battle Monuments Commission chairmen for World Wars I and II. We sign the visitor's book on the table and look around for the old registers from the thirties. They are not in sight. But there is a locked cabinet by the door. Could they be in that?

We walk out to the cemetery where 468 crosses stand on smooth, emerald lawns, manicured as only English lawns are. Red rhododendrons are in full bloom along the clay path leading up to the small memorial chapel, a simple building in the classic style constructed of Portland limestone. Using the card that the War Department gave Grannie in 1930, I quickly locate Percy's cross: Block A, Row 4, Grave 14:

Percy A. Stevens
Pvt. 20 Engrs.
Oregon Feb. 5, 1918.

The cross next to Percy's is inscribed,

Here Rests in Honored Glory
A Comrade in Arms
Known But to God

Graves and chapel in the American cemetery at Brookwood England.
(Author's collection.)

Half of the twenty-four *Tuscania* dead buried at Brookwood are "Known But to God." Up by the chapel a man is changing a sprinkler. He is Denis McGarry, one-time full corporal in the Somerset Light Infantry. Trim and tanned, McGarry has been superintendent of this American cemetery since 1949. I explain that I would like to look at the old registers.

"What years, Sir?"

"The thirties."

"I've been here thirty years, Sir, and I don't remember any that old."

"There must be registers going back that far."

"I don't think so, Sir. Not to my knowledge. Not here."

"Where would they be, then?"

"Oh I don't know, Sir."

I press on in the face of Corporal McGarry's implacable pessimism. "Maybe they are in that cabinet."

"Oh I don't think so, Sir."

"I tried the door. It's locked. Do you have a key?"

"Oh, yes, Well—" not hopefully, "we'll have a look."

We all troop to the visitor's room. McGarry takes out a bunch of keys and tries one in the door of the cabinet. There are half a dozen bound albums inside. McGarry does not bat an eye. "What year did you say you were interested in, Sir?"

"1930."

He places a book on the table and flips the pages.

Joan puts out her hand. "There it is. I saw her name. Go back a page."

Gold Star Mother's signatures in visitor's book at Brookwood cemetery in England for 1 July 1930. Grannie's (Laura Stevens's) is next to last. (Author's collection.)

He does. The page is dated 1 July 1930. The pilgrims' names are down the left side. Opposite them under "Remarks" most of the women have written only "Mother." One from Mississippi has written, "Brookwood brought to me satisfaction and peace." Grannie's remarks are the lengthiest: "Mother, Bend, Oregon. A most beautiful spot for our dear ones laid away brings us comfort and happiness. Thanks to the British government." Beneath her words, "A.C.N." from California has written an anchoritic epitaph: "Where sin cannot touch."

Inside the chapel, inscribed on the marble walls under narrow stained-glass windows, are the names of 563 soldiers and sailors who were lost in waters around the British Isles. Among them are nineteen from the *Tuscania*. On the lintel over the massive bronze doors I read, "Death Hath Not Touched The Spirit Which Remaineth Changeless Forever." I walk back out into the May sunshine and stand again by Percy's cross. That sentiment reminds me of the anodyne my father wrote to grandmother in 1918 after he had learned of "Pike's" death: "He will always be just the same age, never growing older, and the same bright spirit, never changing." I take out the photograph that Grannie carried over here on her pilgrimage fifty years ago, a miniature of the one that hung by her gold star. Yes, for me, too, always the same age, always seventeen. But for me, sixty years later, after another world war, after Korea, after Vietnam, there is little consolation in these words. Only a sadness. I bid a silent farewell to Percy and his comrades who so long ago departed for those "regions unknown." My pilgrimage has ended.

BIBLIOGRAPHY

This book was written for the general reader, not for the scholar; therefore the text was not annotated. But for the history buff here is a list of principle sources. Most of my facts about the torpedoing of the *Tuscania* and the events immediately following were taken from contemporary newspaper accounts. Mr. Lauer's unpublished book was my source for the Royal Navy's rescue operations. Newspapers and the Congressional Record provided me with the bulk of my information about the Gold Star Mothers legislation and pilgrimages. And of course I used family letters and faded newspaper clippings.

"A.W." "The *Tuscania* Dead." *Literary Digest*, 27 April 1918.

The American Battle Monuments Commission. *American Memorials and Overseas Military Cemeteries*. Washington, D.C., 1970.

American Gold Star Mothers, Inc. *Bulletin*. November 1937.

American Legion Monthly. March 1927; July, October 1929.

Andrews, Mary Raymond Shipman. "A Call to Arms." *Scribner's Magazine*, July 1918.

Brogan, Phil. *East of the Cascades*. Portland: Binford and Mort, 1964.

Cameron, Archibald. *Souvenir Album of the Tuscania Disaster*. [Bowmore, Isle of Islay, 1918].

The Congressional Record, 1919-1933.

Department of Transportation, *Hypothermia and Cold Water Survival*, U.S. Coast Guard, n.d.

Dolph, E. A. *Sound Off!* New York: Farrar and Rinehart, 1929.

Du Puy, William A. "Pilgrimages of Mothers to Europe's War Graves." *New York Times*, 23 February 1930.

East Bay Water Company. *Bubbles*. Oakland, California. October 1918.

Ginsburg, Robert. "This, Too, is America." *American Legion Monthly*, November 1933.

Harpham, Josephine Evans. "The Night the Tuscania Went Down." *Oregon Historical Quarterly*, 77 (September 1976).

Hurley, Patrick J. *Pilgrimages for the Mothers and Widows of the American Forces Now Interred in the Cemeteries in Europe*. House Document No. 140, U.S. Government Printing Office. Washington, D.C., 1930.

Lauer, Edward T., Sr., and Leo V. Zimmermann, "The *Tuscania* Disaster." (Unpublished loose-leaf binder collection of Tuscania memorabilia, author's collection.)

Mitchell, Roslyn. "The Two Crusaders." *The Ileach*. Bowmore, Isle of Islay, May 1917.

Noll, John, J. "Crosses." *American Legion Monthly*, September 1930.

The Pilot. Bend High School. Bend, Oregon, 1917.

Smith, Donald A., "Seven Years Ago: The *Tuscania*," *American Legion Weekly*, 30 January 1925.

Stuart, Malcolm. "Legend of Sunken War Dollars to be Tested." *The Guardian*, 25 February 1981.

Wilhelmn, Donald. "A Piece of Paper." *Good Housekeeping*, May 1917.

NEWSPAPERS

Bend Bulletin, 1917-1933.

Bend Methodist, 17 February 1918.

Bulletin (Glasgow), 8 February; 16 March 1918.

Daily Record and Mail (Glasgow), 8, 9, 11, 12, 15 February 1918.

Enderby (B.C.), *Press* 14 February 1918.

Evening News (Glasgow), 8, 9, 11 February 1918.

Glasgow Citizen, 8, 9, 12 February 1918.

Glasgow Herald, 8, 9, 13 February 1918.

London Times, 8, 9, 11, 12 February 1918.

New York Times, 1914-1933.

Okanagan Commoner (Armstrong, B.C.), 4 April 1918.

Portland Oregonian, 1918-1930.

Scotsman (Edinburgh), 8, 9, 11 February 1918.

Worcester (Massachusetts) *Telegram*, 13 June 1937.

COLOPHON

The typeface used for both text and display in *Crusade & Pilgrimage* is Sabon. The last typeface designed by one of the twentieth century's foremost designers, Jan Tschichold, Sabon was created in the early 1960s. Sabon was intended to meet specific pre-photocomposition era technical requirements. A group of German master printers commissioned Tschichold to execute the nearly impossible task of creating a "harmonized" typeface with identical forms for mechanical (Monotype and Linotype) and foundry composition. The successful resultant face, Sabon, is highly readable and pleasing to the eye.

Crusade & Pilgrimage is printed on 80 lb. Shasta Suede with geranium-colored Papan Homespun endsheets. The 12 pt. C1S Springhill cover is foil-stamped and laminated.

The production of *Crusade & Pilgrimage* was accomplished through the cooperation and professional skill of the following persons and firms:

Typesetting:	Irish Setter
Color separations:	Cascade Color
Paper:	The Unisource Corporation
Printing:	Print Tek West
Binding:	Lincoln & Allen Company
Cover photography:	Alan Hicks
Cartography:	John Tomlinson

Designed and produced by the Oregon Historical Society Press.